Living in El Salvador

A Nebraska Farm Boy Joins the Peace Corps

H. LYNN BECK

Ordering Information:
You may search this book in Amazon, Barnes & Nobles and other
online retailers by searching using the ISBN below.

ISBN (Paperback): 978-1-956742-74-9
ISBN (Hardback): 978-1-956742-75-6

Table of Contents

For the people of Puerto Rico and El Salvador, who tolerated my ignorance and helped me to speak Spanish and understand their lives.

Third Edition

Chapter 1

The Decision to Join the Peace Corps

One Saturday I left my dormitory room at the University of Nebraska at Lincoln. I was bored, so I decided to walk around campus. I was in front of the student union when I saw a sign positioned to catch the attention of students entering the building: A Peace Corps representative was interviewing in a basement room.

My curiosity was tickled. I entered the student union and found the interviewing room. It was a small room with a small table and two chairs: one occupied by the Peace Corps interviewer and the other by a student. The interviewer had placed four chairs against the wall, with two people already sitting in these chairs. I occupied a third chair.

When it was my turn to talk to the representative, I gave him a condensed version of my background. He was enthusiastic, especially about my farming experience. He said the Peace Corps had unfilled positions in agriculture and that my skills would be useful in several programs. His excitement made me excited. I was an ordinary Nebraska farm boy. I felt satisfaction that the Peace Corps might need my skills.

During the summer, I felt compelled to be at home to help on the family farm. This included every weekend during the spring and fall farming season, and to any university vacation. My frustration was that I wanted to gain experience doing other things. I had friends who worked in plant nurseries, and for university professors' laboratories—all offering skills that might be useful one day, but I could not disappoint my family. I always needed to return to the family farm. My dissatisfaction grew each year. Another ten years working on the farm was not going to make me more valuable to anyone, nor would it satisfy my need to learn new things.

At the end of my conversation with the Peace Corps representative, I signed up to become a Peace Corps volunteer. As the semester's work intensified, I forgot about my chance encounter with the Peace Corps representative. I told no one about what I had done, and the memory quickly faded.

The semester ended, and I returned for another summer on the farm. I was less than enthusiastic, but it was my duty. After all, the farm generated the revenue that paid my university fees, and I made more money from farming than I could have made from any regular job. There was no doubt about that.

As soon as I arrived on the farm, a letter arrived from the Peace Corps. They invited me to train for their program in El Salvador. My assignment, if I accepted it, would involve teaching peasants to read and write and to help the same peasants produce and market vegetables. I was thrilled. I felt needed, even if I knew nothing about producing vegetables, or teaching people to read and write.

Days later, I still had not told anyone. I wanted to make my decision without anyone telling me why it was my duty to stay on the farm and help the family. I did not need people attempting to influence my decision by making me feel guilty. This was a major decision, and I needed to make it on my own.

I did not need a map to locate El Salvador. I knew precisely where it was, thanks to my sixth-grade teacher. I went to our encyclopedia to learn more about the country. It was extremely poor, heavily populated, and mountainous, with a large Indigenous population. The encyclopedia showed photographs of beautiful, perfectly formed volcanoes. While I viewed the photographs, I reread the Peace Corps invitation. They needed me and I needed them.

I tried to imagine what it would be like to be a Peace Corps volunteer in El Salvador. Would I have running water or electricity? What kind of food would I eat? Would I be able to do what they asked of me? Would I be able to learn to speak Spanish? Could I stay away from home for the length of the Peace Corps contract: twenty-seven months. It consisted of three months training plus twenty-four months of service.

I had no idea what I wanted, but I did know that I did not want to return to the university and that I did not want to continue my life without making drastic changes. If I were not attending the university, I would have to be on the farm, working. My family expected it of me. In my mind, the consequences of not returning to the farm were unthinkable. I was boxed in, except ... I could join the Peace Corps. It was only five years old and everyone in the country knew of it and had a favorable opinion of it. If I left for the Peace Corps, I felt that I could leave the farm without anyone being angry with me.

I checked the box, accepting the assignment, and mailed the return envelope. I had made my decision. Now, I had to digest what I had just done and prepare for the inevitable drama. Little did I know how checking that box would influence the rest of my life. The farm boy who would leave to join the Peace Corps would disappear and an adventurer would replace him, one who always needed to see and work in another country.

After a week of self-reflection, I told my mother. She went silent on me. That was what she did when she was not happy. She won most arguments using this technique. When Mom went silent, you stayed out of her way. Most people figured it was not worth it to try to convince her to change her view, and Mom always won, but she did not win this time. I had made my decision. She played her trump card, but it did not work. Before accepting final defeat, she reminded me that I still had to tell Dad. She expected he would put his foot down and I would return with my head down and again do what they told me.

It was Sunday, and Dad was driving to inspect a farm we owned, located five miles north of our home. I thought this would be a suitable time to tell him. It had rained the night before, and rain took the pressure off farmers and put them in a good mood. In addition, Sundays were not as hectic as the other days. We tried to work only four or five hours on Sunday, mostly irrigating. Dad wanted to see how much rain had fallen on that farm so he could better allocate laborers on Monday.

Dad grabbed his pipe with one hand and while he drove with his knees, he dipped it into his tobacco pouch. He packed the tobacco into his pipe with his thumb, struck a match with his thumbnail, and lit the tobacco with its flame. He drew four or five quick puffs to pull the fire deep into the tobacco, and he tamped the tobacco again with his calloused

3

thumb. The aroma of the tobacco filled the pickup and provided a more relaxed environment. This gave me that extra confidence I needed.

I took a deep breath and said, "Dad, I've decided to join the Peace Corps." I braced for his attack. There was none.

After three or four long puffs on his pipe, he said, "I know. Where are you going?" When I told him, he said, "When will you leave?" I told him. There was no more conversation, only the sound of his drawing on his pipe. The smoke had a calming effect on two people deep in thought.

The rest of the trip was silent, but strangely, it was not tense. It was peaceful. Dad and I had a deep connection that I did not understand. Years later, I learned that during the worst part of the Great Depression, Dad had bought a used Harley-Davidson motorcycle. A friend also had bought one, and they drove through twenty-seven states during the winter. He told me that he was never as cold as when he was in the desert at night. He and his friend tried to keep warm by finding and confiscating old wooden fence posts. They used gasoline from their cycles to start fires to stay warm. That was his attempt at finding adventure.

He told me that he had sold corn for pennies a bushel to finance his trip. This showed me that his adventure had great meaning to him. The trip, paid for with cheap corn, made the trip a very costly one. His posture, and the hint of a smile on a face that seldom smiled, told me that he did not regret his decision made so many years ago. Dad was also an adventurer.

For years, I did not understand how Dad knew that I had applied for the Peace Corps. Now, I know. The application form required three letters of recommendation; one of these was from my hometown banker. He was also my father's banker. This banker and Dad had known each other for decades. When they spoke, it was not always about the weather and loans. I am certain the banker mentioned my request for a letter of recommendation, thinking that Dad already knew. I find it revealing that dad did not share this information with Mom or ask me about it. I can only surmise that he wanted me to have the same chance to make my decision, as he had so many years ago about his great adventure.

After I told Mom and Dad, word spread quickly throughout the neighborhood. Everyone asked me when I was leaving, where I was going, and what I would be doing. It was exciting, but it also became tiresome. I tired of answering the same questions dozens of times, but it was comforting that the community cared so much.

I tried to imagine what things I would need while on my assignment and started to buy them, but there was one problem: it all had to fit into one small trunk. Since most people in Central America were much smaller than the typical American, I needed to buy enough clothes for twenty-seven months, because I would not likely be able to buy any clothes in my size, especially shoes, once I arrived in El Salvador.

We had a family dinner the last weekend before I left. Grandma and Grandpa Tyler and my uncles, aunts, and cousins were all there. These family dinners were always boisterous, with children running about playing. The women took turns yelling at the children to stop and be good. The men were in a corner, telling stories and laughing. Grandma hurried about with her apron on, baking things and making coffee, while Mom or an aunt set the table. Everyone was talking. The men, of which I was not yet a member, stood by a bar improvised from a card table and made themselves drinks while antagonizing me for not being old enough to drink.

Grandpa sat in his easy chair in a corner—his health had limited his mobility for many years. He had his old, deaf hunting dog, Rex, by his side. Rex never left Grandpa's side except for his short visits outside for his necessities. Family members paid their respects, one at a time. It was an honor to have a short conversation with Grandpa. He was not very talkative, but he always listened, and he enjoyed those days as much as the rest of us.

Time passed, and the day arrived for me to leave. It was a weekday, and we left home at four o'clock, which on the farm was the middle of the afternoon. It was strange seeing Dad clean and dressed up. Usually, "dressed up" for Dad was a clean pair of newer overalls, but today he was wearing dress slacks and had shaved and used shaving lotion. I felt guilty taking him from the fields before quitting time, but I felt that Mom did not have to force him from the fields to see me off. Dad felt a bit of envy about my upcoming adventure.

Everyone piled into the car. It was a forty-five-minute drive from the farm to Grand Island. No one spoke during the trip, which created an uncomfortable silence. We arrived at the airport, I checked in, and then

I waited with my family for the airline to call my flight. The wait, like the drive to the airport, was clumsy and seemed never to end. It was an exceedingly small airport, so when the airline called the flight, an airline employee yelled at us over the counter and told us that we had better go to gate two; the plane was boarding passengers.

I hugged everyone and then walked through the gate onto the tarmac, out to the plane, and up the stairs. I took a windowless back seat in the plane, which was an old two-engine turboprop plane. I knew it would be twenty-seven months before I would see my family again. The Peace Corps did not allow trainees and volunteers to return home during those months, except for family emergencies. A dozen other passengers boarded the plane. No one sat near me, which was fine by me. I looked down when the flight attendant asked if I wanted anything. I only shook my head. I did not want her to see my tears or hear my shaky voice.

I flew to Lincoln, then to Omaha, back to Lincoln, and finally to Kansas City. I arrived at ten thirty that night. I spent the night roaming the empty airport, sitting in random chairs, and worrying about what was about to unfold. With eight hours to spend in an empty airport, my imagination took over and made me question my decision. I was scared. I was glad no one was there to see me pace back and forth. The next morning, my flight left at six o'clock for Chicago and then went on to Philadelphia. I was already exhausted.

Chapter 2

My Introduction to the Peace Corps

Processing in Philadelphia

After landing in Philadelphia, I made my way to the Hotel Sylvania, where we would spend three days obtaining visas and vaccinations, signing documents, and attending informational meetings. I entered the hotel and registered. When I reached for the key to go to my room, a bellhop grabbed it and my bags and started toward the elevator. No one had ever carried anything for me in my life. I was a farm boy. I had carried loads heavier than that since I was ten years old. He insulted me. I tried to retake possession of my bags and room key, but the bellhop was ready for that move and avoided my lunge. We entered the elevator, where silence reigned as the elevator carried us to my floor. He opened the door to my room and deposited my bag on the floor, threw my room key onto a table, and put his hand out for a tip. I was ready for that. I grabbed it, gave it a good shake, and thanked him. Now, I had insulted him. Somehow, that made my day better.

I thought Philadelphia was a dirty city. It was crowded with much noise and shouting in the streets. I did not understand how people could tolerate it. Philadelphia's noise was without purpose. It did not have the melody of a diesel engine pulling a heavy load or of a combine swallowing row of corn, husking the ears, separating the cobs from the kernels, and spitting out what it did not need. That was not noise but a symphony. Philadelphia was noisy, and no one seemed to know or respect anyone. I did not like it at all. I could not imagine anyone wanting to live there or even pass through it unless obliged to do so.

Finally, we signed all the papers, filled out all forms, and received all the vaccinations, and I was on the move again, but this time it was with my fellow trainees. The unknown was not so formidable when confronted as a group. We climbed onto buses for our trip into New York City and on to the airport. From the airport, we would fly on to three months' training in Puerto Rico. The drive from Philadelphia to New York City revealed another dirty and noisy city. I had never seen so many people, and I had never wanted to be somewhere else so much as during that short trip.

After the usual formalities, we found our plane to San Juan and boarded. When the door shut on the plane and the flight attendant locked it, I knew the next time it opened I would be in Puerto Rico. That would be the first time I would be outside the continental United States. I had wondered for years what it would be like to stand in a tropical land and to breathe tropical air. Within hours, I would have my answer.

We arrived in Puerto Rico. The flight attendant cracked the door on the plane allowing the tropical air to enter the cabin. When I approached the door to descend to the tarmac, the sea breeze and high humidity hit me. The air smelled different. I could not describe the difference, but there was one. We deplaned, found our luggage, and moved into the waiting US Navy buses to start our long trip from San Juan to Arecibo (ah-ray-*see*-bow).

Arecibo was a regional city located on the northwest coast of Puerto Rico. There was so much to see as the bus made its way west that I tried not to blink. I looked at the palm trees, the coconut trees, and all the people in the streets. The people were everywhere. Their clothes were colorful and tight. They seemed happy to be alive, unlike anybody I had seen in Philadelphia or New York—those were angry people.

The houses were also vastly different. They were made of brick that had a coating of a plaster-like material over it. The windows were jalousie windows—louvered glass that opened and closed like window blinds. Roofs made from tile were all reddish-brown. In addition, the traffic was crazy. It seemed to me that no one obeyed traffic laws, if there actually were any.

Our Camp at the Top of a Mountain in a Rain Forest

Everyone was excited when we arrived in the city of Arecibo. It felt like we were on a bus filled with eight-year-olds on a sugar high. We moved about the empty seats and looked out the windows. The buses were making their way through the city, and then we entered a highway that led out of town. We started to climb. There were sharp curves, making it slow going as we climbed higher and higher. The road narrowed even more until it became little more than a one-lane road. What looked like a youth camp appeared; the road stopped; the buses stopped. Our leaders asked us to gather our luggage and follow the driver to the administrative building. We had arrived.

We received our bunkhouse assignments. I followed the crushed-rock path until I found mine. It was on the downside of the mountain slope. I entered and waited for my eyes to adjust to the darkness. A few trainees were already there, up righting bunk beds and straightening chairs. I found an acceptable bed, pushed it against the wall, and laid out my things. The mattresses smelled musty from disuse and high humidity. We returned to the administration building for further instructions. That was when we learned that we were training with another trainee group that was going to the Dominican Republic.

Management told us we had to be at the basketball court promptly at 6:00 a.m., ready for calisthenics, A former US Marine would lead us in rigorous physical training until 7:00 a.m., at which time we would have thirty minutes to return to our bunkhouses, shower, change clothes, shave, and do whatever else we had to do. Breakfast was from 7:30 to 8:00.

Our classes started promptly at 8:00 a.m. and continued until 8:00 p.m., with a short break for lunch and dinner. After which our teachers expected us to study for our next day's Spanish classes. We covered one chapter each day from a university textbook. The instructors handed out the Spanish textbook and a Spanish-to-English/ English-to-Spanish dictionary to their students. The dictionary would never leave my side for the next twelve months.

Other classes included community development, gardening, and a host of other things. We received our classroom assignments. Class size was no more than five per instructor, with all classes composed of trainees with a similar level of Spanish knowledge.

The staff constantly observed us. When the staff noticed a characteristic that would contribute to a trainee being unsuccessful, they assigned points to that trainee. The more serious the infraction, the more points assigned. When the head trainer totaled these points from all staff members, he decided if the trainee should continue to train or if the trainee should be released.

The staff members were all highly trained. They understood what we would face in-country. Their goal was to help us become successful. Unsuccessful trainees could embarrass themselves and the Peace Corps. Some people, through no fault of their own, were not wired to live successfully in another culture. These candidates were the ones the staff sought to *deselect* (remove from the program). Every trainee feared being deselected. We quickly became aware that the purpose of training was not only to teach us Spanish but to find the trainees who did not fit the Peace Corps mold and deselect them.

The first week was full of excitement as we became accustomed to our new routines; the East and West Coast activists, however, were not happy with our physical-training activities. They voiced their concerns to the camp manager, but he did not give them what they wanted, so they went over his head. They discovered who his boss was in Washington, DC, and began drafting a document to the camp manager's boss to repeal the daily physical workout. They worked late into the night for three nights. They always huddled around a table in the cafeteria, drinking coffee. I noted that all of the ad hoc committee members had long hair and long beards. I surmised that this was not their first protest. They finished their document and sent it off to Washington, and we all waited breathlessly for the response.

As part of our training, we formed a cooperative to provide small items like toothpaste, soap, and deodorant. Each trainee was a member of the cooperative. We would receive a dividend at the end of training in proportion to how much we spent buying co-op goods. A staff member went into Arecibo and bought shampoo, toothpaste and toothbrushes, gum, candy, alcohol, and other necessities. We added a small markup, and then we sold it to ourselves. The cantina was open for thirty minutes in the afternoon and again, briefly, after classes ended at night.

One of our trainees had an enterprising spirit—a businessperson always looking for an economic opportunity that he could exploit. He looked at the way we operated the co-op, and he saw opportunity. He knew that he could buy these articles and others in the Virgin Islands, tax-free. Every two or three weeks, he paid a trainee's travel expenses to take a weekend outing in the Virgin Islands. All the trainees had to do was to buy the things on our businessperson's shopping list and bring them back to camp. Our entrepreneur had a much better selection of items, and his prices were just below those of the coop. If someone wanted a candy bar or anything else during the day, the businessperson was glad to walk him to his bunk, open his magical suitcase, and close the sale.

Within thirty days, the co-op was out of business, and our entrepreneur's business had turned into a monopoly. We learned two lessons: government was not as good at conducting business as businesspeople were, and co-ops, if not effectively managed, could fail.

I struggled with learning Spanish. I tried to learn it, but it was mostly Greek to me; still, my vocabulary increased very slowly, as did my conversational ability. I had taken a Spanish class during my first semester at the university, but three weeks into the semester, the instructor came to me and said, "Not everyone has the ability to learn a foreign language;" he handed back another quiz with a grade of F. I dropped the class. From that moment, I had a nagging doubt if I could learn a foreign language.

Within a week, we heard the decision about the obligatory hour of exercise at 6:00 a.m. The Peace Corps agreed to make it optional. From that point, no one showed up for exercises. Everyone chose to sleep one more hour.

Week by week, my Spanish improved a little, but I was still horrible at it. I was in the bottom level with other people like me. I knew they watched us because we would have to make significant gains each day to become Peace Corps volunteers at the end of three months. The Peace Corps wanted to identify people unlikely to learn enough Spanish to survive by themselves in our host country. Sometimes this required that the Peace Corps cut its losses. I knew this because the staff deselected one woman in her sixties after three weeks' training due to inadequate progress in Spanish. They offered her another position in an English-speaking country. I was very worried that I might be next. I could not allow that outcome. I had to learn Spanish and make it to El Salvador.

August 7, 1967, Puerto Rico—First Field Trip

One night, we had a meeting for all trainees going to El Salvador. The staff gave each of us a packet. Inside the packet was a highway map of Puerto Rico with an X marking a spot on a road—a different spot for each trainee. Our assignment was to make our way from Arecibo to that point on the highway, find a Puerto Rican family to house and feed us for three days and nights, and learn as much as possible about the community. For our needs, the Peace Corps gave us four dollars a day for occasional expenditures and transportation to and from that location. We could not use any of our own money for any purpose. We were to speak only Spanish. The violation of any of these rules would result in our being terminated from the program and returned to the US. Within this period, someone from the Peace Corps would visit us on site. They would interview people in the area to learn if we had violated any of these rules and to evaluate our performance.

After the meeting, I went to one of the open classrooms and sat. I was frightened. I had received three weeks of Spanish classes, yet I could not converse in Spanish, and my level of understanding Spanish conversation was minimal—almost zero. My level of confidence could not have been lower. I did not want to be deselected.

The next morning everyone was up early, except for a few stragglers. The stragglers had nothing to worry about because they already knew how to speak Spanish. We had to be in the vans and ready to roll by 7:30 a.m. By 7:35, we were packed and stacked in the back. We needed one more van than we had. They compensated the lack of van seating by adding two or three more trainees to each of our vans. We were like cattle in a cattle truck.

A carpenter had made benches from wooden planks and covered them with foam. There was one plank on each side of the van, and another located just behind the front seat. Everyone tried to avoid the plank behind the front seat. That meant riding backward up and down the mountain; these riders tended to develop motion sickness.

The trip from our rain forest mountain camp to the city of Arecibo was a long and winding one. There were curves that, when taken too fast, threw the riders on one side of the van into the passengers riding on the other side of the van. In those days, there were no seat belts. We were unsecured ballast.

As we descended the mountain, the other trainees sang songs. I did not sing—ever. My mood was one of pure fright. The Peace Corps was transporting me into the unknown. My colleagues were all at least two years older than I was and had university degrees; most had graduated from well-known universities. Many had spent a summer backpacking through Europe, and they had had at least two years of a foreign language in high school, with additional training in college. Even though I had had two years at the university, I never again attempted to take a language course after my first fiasco. Mentally, I had never left the farm. Now, I was so far out of my comfort zone that I did not know if I could find my way back. I felt inferior to the other trainees.

They dropped us at an American restaurant in the center of Arecibo. From there, we were supposed to find our way to our separate destinations. The limited money they gave us ensured that we would not take taxis anywhere. Most trainees were nervous and divided into small groups, filling the restaurant. I stayed by myself at the counter and ordered a Coke. That was a treat, and it was so very cold, just the way I liked it. I sipped it slowly and worried about my next step.

It was eleven in the morning, and most of us were still hanging around the restaurant. I had consumed all the Coke I could afford. I had to move, or I would not reach my destination during daylight, which would result in my immediate deselection. I asked the English-speaking waiter where I should go to start my journey. After thinking and asking another waiter, he explained that it was a mile or so to a particular street in a residential neighborhood. The spot I was seeking consisted of a couple of cars parked along the street, where they waited for people to fill their cars. The drivers serviced a couple of rural villages, one being where I needed to go. I did not understand why there was no central bus system. In Arecibo, the city had decentralized the buses and taxis. Why the cars going to those villages decided to park on that street must have been an interesting story.

I decided to avoid the expense and complication of finding a bus that would take me from the restaurant to where the cars were waiting; I would walk and carry my duffel bag. I fretted the entire time. I approached what I thought was the correct street and looked for a car. Looking for a parked car in a residential area was not reassuring to me. I expected to see cars parked everywhere, but there were three cars parked—which one would take me to the X on my map, and which ones belonged to a specific house?

Finally, I saw a parked car with a couple of people hanging around and conversing. I mentally rehearsed my Spanish, but I did not know which person to approach. Finally, one walked around to the driver's door and reached inside to grab a cigarette. I approached him and asked if he drove to my destination. There was confusion, and the other person joined in, attempting to understand me. Eventually, the driver said yes. I thought I understood that I was to wait, so I waited.

After waiting ten minutes, I did not understand why we had not left yet. I again attempted to ask if he was going to my destination. He confirmed and pointed to the back seat, so I sat. Soon, a woman appeared and sat beside me, forcing me into the middle of the back seat. Little by little, people appeared with packages, and the back seat filled and then the front seat. The driver packed the car. There were four of us in the back seat and three in the front seat, each with our things. The driver started the car, and we left. I was at once relieved and scared.

We left the narrow streets of the city and entered a lush green countryside. Puerto Rico was an exceptionally beautiful country. I loved staring at it and all its hues of green and blue. We reached a fork in the road and turned left and then another fork, and we turned right. All the time, I wondered if the driver had really understood me and was taking me to the place I wanted to go. I had no idea how much he was going to charge me. Would I have enough money? The driver stopped repeatedly, and people left the car with their packages. It was great having more room in the car. Finally, the car stopped, and the driver pointed to me and motioned that I should leave the car. We were nowhere. We were in the middle of a valley with no houses visible. The driver put his hand out and told me the price. It seemed reasonable; I paid him, and he drove off. I was nowhere, by myself, clueless—and one second from panicking and having a meltdown. I could not just sit down and cry, but I wanted to.

Finally, I picked a direction, grabbed my luggage, and started walking. After a bit, I saw a mile marker. It was not even close to where I should have been. I did not even know if I was on the right highway. I looked at the sky and thought that rain was about to fall. I was desperate. A car approached. I flagged it down. The driver kindly stopped. He had a passenger. I tried to speak Spanish, but they did not understand me. The passenger tried to speak English, but I could not understand him. This made him angry because he saw no reason that I should not understand him. The driver intervened. I showed him my X on the map. He motioned me to get into his car. I did, and within ten minutes, we came into a cluster of houses. He stopped in front of a *tienda*, which is a small store, often located in a single-car garage—a Latin convenience store. Families used *tiendas* to supplement the family's income by selling essential products.

The driver motioned for me to get out. I did. I thanked him, paid him, and he was off. He was kind to me when I needed kindness. He did not have to stop to help me.

It was three o'clock, and I had not eaten since breakfast, other than the multiple Cokes I had drunk in Arecibo. I did not know what to do, so I drew a deep breath and entered the *tienda*. Before speaking, I rehearsed what I thought I needed to say. When the man behind the counter finished waiting on other people, he turned his eyes toward me. They held no expression, and he asked no question. He just stared at me, frowning. I gave him my best Spanish, and a Pepsi appeared over the counter. I smiled internally. He extended his hand. I asked how much. He answered in English. That worried me because I had to speak Spanish, or the staff would deselect me and return me to the US. I paid and stepped outside to sip my soda, biding my time before I had to start begging for a place to stay.

After I finished my drink, it was time for me to find a homeowner who would accept me into his home and feed me for three days. I walked up to the first house. It had to belong to a person with above-average income for the neighborhood because it was much larger than the other houses, and a high wall surrounded the property. I thought this house would offer my best chance. I walked up to the outer fence and rang the bell. After a long pause, an expressionless maid appeared and stared at me. I tried to explain to her what I needed. The maid had no idea what I was saying and made no attempt to understand. She held out her upright palm, indicating I should wait. She closed the door and disappeared. A minute later, I heard someone approaching. A woman opened the door and looked at me. I used my best Spanish to ask her to let me live with her family for three days—a task that took great courage on my part. She said nothing but wagged her index finger back and forth as a definite no. She backed up and closed the door.

She had looked upset that I had brought her into my problem. Really, why would a middle-aged housewife tell a twenty-year-old male American—a stranger—that he could live in her house with her husband and children? If she had, her husband would have been furious. It was not for her to decide such things; only the man could decide, and he was at work.

I went from house to house, asking the same question—a question to which I knew the answer. I knew I was putting these families in an inconvenient situation. Not surprisingly, everyone gave the same answer.

To lick my wounds and build my confidence, I walked down the road in the direction that led out of the village. I wanted to see what was there. On the edge of the village, a couple of blocks beyond the last house, I saw an old, abandoned house. It had no door or windows, and one-third of the roof was missing. I ventured inside and saw that it consisted of one large room, which was mostly dry. It offered protection from weather events, especially if it did not rain. I looked out the window frames in the back of the house and saw a most picturesque view. Puerto Rico was beautiful. It was a dreamland. If I found no place to stay this night, I decided that I would return here for comfort and try again tomorrow. I was like a homeless stray puppy.

Toward the end of the day, I noticed that I had visited all the village's houses except for three. They were located high on the hill above the road. I decided I needed more time before I approached them. I returned to the *tienda*, overcame my concern for conserving my living allowance, and ordered another Pepsi. This time, fearing that I might not have supper, I added a candy bar to my order. I was famished. I looked at my watch and saw that it was a quarter to six. The sun was fading. I knew that it would be dark by six o'clock. In this region, there was almost no dusk. It was light, and then it was dark.

I finished my snack and headed up the hill to the first house. I told myself that if I were unable to convince one of the three families to take me in, I would have no other choice but to return to the abandoned house and settle in for the night.

My heart sank a little as I visited each house, and each time they denied my request, although in a kind way. The Puerto Rican people were always kind to me. When they told me that they could not accept me, they were respectful and genuinely sad. I knew that what I was asking was difficult for them to grant.

These families were very low-income families who barely had enough to eat. Their houses were small. To allow a stranger into their homes would mean that someone would sleep on the floor, and etiquette would not allow that to be me. They did not have doors on their rooms; therefore, they could not isolate themselves inside their rooms and lock the door. In addition, they would be embarrassed if they did not have enough food to offer their guest and for themselves. In addition, they would be subjecting their families to significant risk by asking a stranger into their homes—a foreign stranger. I understood their hesitancy to accept me. I felt horrible having to ask them.

After the last house denied me, I walked down the steep hill, slowly, pensively. I questioned my decision to leave home. Home was boring, but I always had a roof over my head and food to eat. Right then, those two things became particularly important. I decided I would return to the *tienda* and find something to serve as food and then return to the abandoned house for the night. As I descended the hill and approached the road, a car appeared.

Upon seeing me in his high beams, the driver screeched to a stop. He reached over, threw open the passenger door, and yelled, "I hear you are looking for a place to stay. Come on; get in." Yes, he said it in English, but I did not care. I got in and waited for him to explain.

He said that there was talk in the village about the poor stranger looking for a place to stay. They were sorry they could not accept me into their homes. They were embarrassed to have a stranger, especially an

American, see how little they had. In addition, during the day, the men were working. In Puerto Rico, a woman cannot allow any man to enter her house without the man of the house being present. This could never happen.

The man said that he lived in the next small city with his wife and two young children. They could offer me a rollaway bed, breakfast, and dinner. I almost kissed him. I told him that the Peace Corps expected us always to speak Spanish, and I needed to arrive early in the village and stay there until late. He agreed to help me with my Spanish, take me to the village early, and pick me as he returned home from work. I could not believe my luck. Puerto Ricans were so kind.

This arrangement worked well. My caretakers had family in the village, and they took turns babysitting me. They showed me a coffee *beneficio* (beh-neh-*fee*-see-oh), where they processed coffee from freshly picked beans to dried beans. They showed me enterprise operations for cattle and vegetable and fruit production and how farmers made their livings on ten or fewer acres—some with less than an acre to their names.

By the end of the first field trip, I was building confidence. My Spanish was better, and I had been surviving on my own. I was learning to bridge cultural and speech gaps by incorporating hand signals into my conversations and with heavy use of the bilingual dictionary. I had made great progress, but I had a long way to go. I always had difficulty explaining why I was in Puerto Rico and why I was in their community. They did not let their lack of understanding bother them. They accepted me and did everything they could to help me.

During this first field trip, I had noticed that every house had a photograph of John F. Kennedy. Puerto Ricans adored him. When they learned that JFK was responsible for creating the Peace Corps, they opened their arms and hearts to us, as his representatives. Although people had no idea what the Peace Corps was, they knew and loved JFK. That was enough for them.

When I returned to our camp, I discovered that a dozen of my fellow trainees had come home early, picked up a plane ticket, and returned to the USA. They had experienced demanding situations that they did not know how to manage; they managed it by leaving. Other than the obvious requirement to learn to speak Spanish, a major objective of the Peace Corps was for the trainee to become capable of handling difficult and stressful situations.

August 14, 1967, Puerto Rico—After the First Field Trip

One month into our training, we were all tired because we had been on a fourteen-hours-a-day, six-days-a-week routine. We were in either class or studying from 8:00 a.m. to 10:00 p.m. Our camp director promised us a three-day weekend, which we started to anticipate. The more adventurous trainees had planned a trip to the beach. Then suddenly, the camp director canceled our extended weekend without any explanation. The adventurous ones were already feeling the sand between their toes, the wind in their hair, and the smoke in their pipes. They were unhappy.

I was not ready for the hassle of leaving camp. There was so much that could go wrong with transportation arrangements, and I did not feel secure with my Spanish-speaking ability. I was not ready for those problems and was happy to stay safely in the camp. I did not want to give the staff any reason to deselect me.

Instead of a three-day weekend, the Peace Corps staff decided to take us on a day trip to a place in a rural area. Who was I to judge the soundness of their reasoning? They had experience and knew things we did not know.

We recently had had so many meetings that it was difficult to stay awake. Then, we would have hours of Spanish class. No one was complaining about the Spanish classes; we needed them. We had to contend with so many other community development classes of questionable value. Being exhausted made it difficult to learn Spanish, and we had to do that.

The camp director called a meeting to discuss the growing discontentment. Trainees held the opinion that fewer meetings and shorter days would help because we would have more energy, and we could learn more Spanish, but the camp director drew a line in the sand and told us to measure up or have a good flight home. We were not expecting that. Surprise!

Rumors circulated that all this was a training technique to separate the weak trainees from the strong. They allowed us to have expectations of a wonderful weekend, and then they dashed our hopes at the last moment and had more work for us to do. It did not matter to me. I was not leaving camp unless the staff forced me.

August 18, 1967, Puerto Rico—The Retreat

Management called a meeting. They decided to give us the next Saturday and Sunday off. They arranged for us to spend the weekend at a workers' resort hotel, located east of Ponce (*Pon*-say). Ponce is on the south side of the island. The hotel cost three dollars a night, with six to eight people per room. We were near the beach; plus, the resort had a small swimming pool. Trainees split their time between the beach and the swimming pool, drinking rum and Cokes, and sleeping. Although our stay at the resort was short, it was restful.

August 20, 1967, Puerto Rico—Learn to Be Unoccupied

In our community-development class, the instructor informed us that we would need to learn to be "unoccupied." He said that where we were going, the rainy season lasted six months. During this season, the peasants would be in their fields, working, and it would be unlikely that most peasants would be interested in any of our meetings. He gave an example. There was a married couple in the previous training program, who seemed happy in their marriage. The couple gave the impression that they could cope with anything, but after seven months of service, they divorced and left the program. The trainer insinuated that their divorce was the result of their inability to cope with the boredom. Successful volunteers learned to make boredom their friend by finding something to do until the community needed them again.

Two more people left the program. Our El Salvador group had started with fifty-eight trainees and at this point had eleven fewer. That was almost a 20 percent reduction in the number of trainees after five weeks into our training.

August 28, 1967, Puerto Rico—Field Trip 2

I was again in my field-trip village. Everything was much easier this time, even though my Spanish had not improved much. It just did not click in my head. I felt so stupid. The other trainees were improving faster than I was, except for the married couples. They constantly spoke English with each other, rather than seeking conversation with Spanish- speaking people, and their Spanish suffered for that reason.

I was ashamed to admit it, but there was a moment when I had decided to return to Nebraska after this second field trip. Then I met a man who befriended me. He always spoke Spanish slowly with me. I began to understand more of what he was saying, and I decided to try harder. He took me to visit coffee and sugar plantations, and I saw the greenest and lushest pastures. He even took me through a small coffee *beneficio*. It was interesting. I was impressed that he would take the time to show me these things. He did so in a way that captured my imagination.

We walked up and down hills as he led me through fenced and lush pastures to a small wooden house built on tall stilts. It was high enough that grass grew under it, cattle grazed under it, and we walked under it with no danger of hitting our heads on the house's floor.

We climbed a tall staircase. He shouted to someone inside the house. I learned that this house was his brother-in-law's and sister's. His sister came to greet us with a huge smile. She kissed her brother on both cheeks and extended her hand toward me. She offered us chairs at the kitchen table and started making coffee. I already felt at home. He explained to her my mission, and she retained her smile, as if she was proud of me. She was like the sun, illuminating everything she looked at. She made me seem important. This was from her role of making the Latin male seem important. If so, she filled this role with superb skill. I will never forget the rich flavor of her coffee and the warm feeling I received from both this man and his sister. This was the first time I had felt true friendship from anyone.

The sun was close to setting when we left. We walked faster on the return because I had to catch my ride into the town for my meal and sleeping arrangement. What a wonderful day! The siblings may well have been angels. I had never felt so accepted and understood.

I was waiting for my supervisor to visit me and evaluate me. Finally, she came. She was abrupt in telling me that I could not stay with the same family on my final field trip because I needed to stay with a family that would most closely resemble my living conditions in El Salvador. I had no problem with that. At least she gave me an opportunity to find another family before I returned to camp. I did not know how to tell my kind family that I could not stay with them again because they had a nice shower, a tiled floor, a cement house, and were very educated.

The small farmers that I met were intelligent. They supported a wife and three or four children, sometimes, on less than one acre. At most, the farmers had ten acres. These were the families who lived in the small wooden houses, lit with one or two forty-watt bulbs. I had no idea how their children studied and did their homework at night. Small farmers sometimes performed day labor for larger farmers. I would see them in a field, bent over, weeding around plants. They lived on roads that did not appear to have been used for years, even though they were heavily traveled. The weeds and grass retained possession of the road because foot traffic did slight damage to the vegetation, and any damage that was done quickly repaired itself.

These small farmers did not own a vehicle. Their wives took a bus to town to do their shopping. Sometimes the bus did not pass within a half mile or more of their houses. They had to carry their purchases that far. They needed to go shopping more often than they would have if they had a vehicle because they had to carry whatever they bought. All families had running water in their homes, but few had hot water. I saw one house that was smaller than our living room in Nebraska, and the family had nine children.

One night I had a long talk with a sixteen-year-old boy. He knew much about agriculture. He explained different plant diseases to me. Although my Spanish was still severely limited, I was impressed by how many ways there were to explain something. In fact, my English was improving because of this experience. As I saw more ways to say the same thing in Spanish, I learned more ways to say it in English. The following morning, I visited with an agronomist. After that, I returned to the training camp. I was becoming excited about reaching El Salvador.

September 2, 1967, Puerto Rico—The New York Psychologist

Trainee feelings in the camp were volatile. Mid-boards were over, and they were more important than anyone realized. Management released four more trainees, and with more warned that they were likely to be eliminated before the end of training, which was still six weeks away. The listed reasons for being released (or likely to be released) before training's end were as follows:

1. The trainee was too neat to be able to adjust to living with poor people.
2. The trainee was too sloppy to be able to adjust to living with poor people.
3. The trainee was too immature to be able to adjust to living in another culture.
4. The trainee lacked the socialization skills necessary to adjust to living in another culture.

I was worried about numbers three and four. I was two years younger than any other trainee, and several were six to eight years older than I was. On a good day, my social skills were near zero, although I interacted better with the Puerto Ricans than I did with the Americans.

The Peace Corps had a psychologist who periodically flew in from New York. He came on weekends because he had a regular practice there. He was tall, very heavy, and sported a moustache; he was semi- bald and always wore dark sunglasses and dark, oversized clothes. He reminded everyone of a spy, which he was—for the Peace Corps. He walked around and stopped in odd places, mostly those that were in the shade. I always wondered if he went to the shade for the heat relief or if he thought he was invisible there. He always had a notepad, on which he took copious notes, and then, suddenly, he would move to another spot. We believed he moved every time he thought we discovered his position. I thought he had watched too many spy movies.

He did this all weekend, and then he disappeared from camp about Sunday noon. The psychologist's behavior was far from normal, and we were certain he would have difficulties adjusting to most social settings.

What concerned us was that he sat in judgment of us. We never knew if we were on the verge of being deselected. That was always disconcerting.

Management informed us that our behavior during the last two field trips would account for at least half of our consideration for their selecting us as volunteers. This did not make us feel any better. The tactless psychologist told us that his job was to make us feel insecure and quit the program. Shocked, one trainee asked if he would care to reword his statement. He did not. He repeated what he had just said and asked us if we knew what we were getting ourselves into. He was not only weird; he was mean.

September 9, 1967, Puerto Rico—The Fateful Trip to the Beach

After the tension from the second field trip and the result of our midterm evaluations, our camp director thought that it was time to give us Saturday and Sunday off. The East Coast and West Coast coalition decided they would fulfill their fantasies with a beach party. They arranged for transportation to a beach they had heard about. It was late Friday afternoon.

We did not hear any more from the group until Sunday afternoon, about the time they should have been returning. We spotted excitement around the administration building. We heard that the police had arrested the entire group and were holding them in an Arecibo jail, with deselection from the program the most likely result.

The story, as we heard it, was that they went to the beach that someone had recommended to them for Friday night. They enjoyed the beach but grew tired of it. They sent search parties out on Saturday and found a lovely beach. They decided to move their festivities there early Sunday morning.

They enjoyed their evening partying by drinking, smoking, and doing whatever else healthy young people did in those situations. By morning, they were very drunk or high, many were nude and swimming in the warm waters of the Atlantic Ocean. Meanwhile, not far from the beach, an old man and his wife prepared to have their customary breakfast on their backyard patio, with its unequaled and unobstructed view of the ocean. It was always so peaceful there, and they enjoyed the experience. And that is when things started to go awry.

As Mrs. Old Man carried breakfast out to their patio table on a large tray. She looked up and saw a large group of stumbling, drunk, and nude people doing disgusting things on their private beach. She screamed and dropped her tray. Mr. Old Man ran from inside the house, the best he could with a bad hip, and looked where Mrs. Old Man was pointing a crooked finger with one hand while she grasped her heart with her other hand, almost swooning. He returned inside his house, with his wife in tow. She was attempting to faint but could not because he was pulling her. He sat her down in a comfortable chair, picked up the phone, and started making phone calls. And that was when things went off the rails.

Lickety-split, the police rounded up the misbehaving group and rushed them to jail. As the lack of luck would have it for our stressed- out group of Peace Corps trainees, the old man was on Puerto Rico's Supreme Court; in fact, he was the Chief Justice. When he picked up the phone, he called the head of Puerto Rico's police, the mayor of Arecibo, and the governor of Puerto Rico. These three contacts did the rest for him.

Within minutes, they contacted the State Department and the Peace Corps in Washington, DC, the head administrator of our training camp, and anyone else of any standing in the community or on the island. To say that the proverbial stuff hit the fan would be the understatement of the century.

After a couple of days, they brought our misfits back to camp. The old man wanted them thrown out of the Peace Corps and Puerto Rico. In fact, the Supreme Court Justice would have been happier if the Peace Corps had relocated out of his hemisphere. These unlucky adventurers represented twenty-five percent of remaining trainees. The Peace Corps did not want to lose its investment. Even though they had showed little common sense, these trainees were leaders and could become the most successful Peace Corps volunteers, but it was exactly this type of behavior that could also result in the Peace Corps being embarrassed on the front pages of a country's newspapers and on the evening news on television. It could even result in the Puerto Rican government throwing the Peace Corps from their island. Not everyone would be as understanding and willing to compromise as the old man and his wife in Puerto Rico.

After they repatriated the group with the rest of us in the training camp, the camp director subjected them to a serious scolding before he informed them that they would allow them to finish their training. However, if they even coughed without covering their mouths, they would be on the next flight home. I think after all the attention they received; the group saw the error of their ways.

September 27, 1967, Puerto Rico—Field Trip 3

The party-minded people decided we should have a party before our third and last trip. We all contributed a few bucks to purchase a pig from one of the camp employees. Locals would roast a pig over an open fire. We also hired a steel band, which makes tropical music on instruments made from oil barrels, and local people to prepare the food.

We started eating before dark. They made the punch from pineapple. I did not think that pineapple punch could be tasty, but it was delicious. After eating, I played basketball with a couple of trainees.

They had constructed the basketball court on a wide terrace carved from the steep hillside. They carved one side from the hillside, and the other was filled in to make a narrow basketball court. The problem with the court was that every time that the ball bounced to the downhill side, it rolled downhill until a tree or bush stopped it. It discouraged the most enthusiastic player, but on this night, I was persistent.

I played for a bit, and then I laid the ball carefully on the court to keep it from rolling downhill. I walked to the back door (the closest one) of the cafeteria and passed by the food line until I arrived at the punch bowl. I poured myself a big cup of punch. The taste was that of pineapple, but it had a hint of something unknown to me; I liked whatever it was. I walked out the front side of the cafeteria (now the closest exit for me) and headed back to the basketball court, sipping from my juice cup as I walked.

After a four or five such trips, I noticed that when I shot at the basket, I missed more often. I spent more time chasing the basketball than I did shooting it. As I gained confidence in my basketball skills, however, instead of leaving the ball on the court when I went for more punch, I dribbled the ball past the food line, got my punch, and then dribbled out of the dining hall and back onto the court. Everyone else had long abandoned the court, but I continued to climb down and crawl up the hillside, chasing the ball. During the early morning hours, I finally tired and decided to go to bed. We were starting our trip down the mountain the following morning at seven o'clock for our third and final field trip.

On my way to the cabin, I noticed that no one else was around. The camp seemed abandoned. I started to worry. Had I missed a signal to abandon camp? I entered my bunkhouse; it was empty. Curious, I started walking, although with difficulty, from bunkhouse to bunkhouse. Finally, I found a bunkhouse that had smoke pouring from its screened windows. It was either on fire, or I had found my fellow trainees. They were all sitting on the floor, smoking. I did not smoke, so I returned to my cabin. I looked at my watch; it was five o'clock. The sun would be up in one hour. When I lay down, the cabin started to spin. I could not close my eyes. I had to stand up. I felt uncomfortable. What had been in that pineapple punch?

The next morning, starting at six thirty, the Peace Corps staff went from cabin to cabin, ringing a bell and yelling for us to rise. They reminded us that we were rolling down the mountain at seven o'clock sharp. I felt horrible, but I climbed out of my bed, dressed, threw a few things into my travel bag, and made my way to the loading area. I did not eat. I could not eat; I could not even think about food.

The staff continued to go from cabin to cabin, yelling orders; then the threats started. Any trainee not ready by seven o'clock would have points deducted on their final evaluation score. Slowly, the trainees started to appear. All the trainees looked horrible, including me. Four or five ran to the forest's edge and unceremoniously emptied their stomachs before they could climb into the van. That is when I learned that an evil trainee had emptied several bottles of rum into the pineapple juice. That was the first time I had tasted alcohol. I felt betrayed. How could anything that tasted so good earlier make us feel so bad now? We left closer to seven thirty, but we did leave.

The driver forced us into the back of the vans. In each van, three trainees had the undesirable seats facing backward. Once the doors closed, there was no ventilation. With all trainees loaded, the staff member responsible for driving closed the doors; immediately, the temperature started to rise, and we started to panic. We knew this would not end well.

We began our descent down the mountain. Our convoy consisted of four vans. The road had dozens of ups and downs and curves in the road. Some curves were sharp, tossing us from side to side, and it was becoming hotter in the back of the van. At first, we were surviving, but then someone started gasping and then heaving. We shouted for the driver to stop. We begged him to stop. We did not want the smell of vomit in such a confined place with so many stressed and uncomfortable trainees, but it was too late. Now, more trainees were gasping, and others were already heaving. The situation was critical.

The driver pulled to the side of the road, ran to the back, and threw open the door. He gasped, covered his nostrils, and stepped back in horror. We piled out and sought clean air. More were on the side of the road, grabbing their ankles and heaving, while others were able to recover after a little gagging. Someone had a water jug and tried to wash the damage from the back of the van, but that was only partially successful. We needed more water than that if we were going to erase all the damage.

The other vans drove by, honking, with the trainees laughing and pointing at us. We were too stressed to care.

After the tipsy trainees regained their composure, we reentered the van, and the driver returned to the road. After a mile or two, we passed first one van and then another van, with their trainees lined up at the road's edge, grabbing their ankles. The vans played hopscotch with each other all the way into Arecibo. When one van was on the edge of the road, the others passed, but there was no more laughing or honking. We were in survival mode. That was the longest and most uncomfortable trip I have made in my life.

We arrived in Arecibo at nine o'clock. The drivers delivered us to the American restaurant in the center of town. All but two of the staff left to spend a couple of hours shopping in town before returning to camp. The two staff members were to monitor our progress.

We trainees were supposed to start our trip to the country immediately. We did not. We entered the American restaurant and sat at the counter or claimed a table with our heads hanging. We took turns going into the restroom to wash our faces and rinse our mouths after a new round of heaving.

After a half of hour sitting at the counter with my head leaning heavily on my hands, I ordered a Coke. I drank it slowly. I started to feel better. The Coke settled my stomach. At ten o'clock, staff members returned to check on us. They were not happy when they found us exactly where they had left us. No one—not one trainee—had vacated the restaurant. They reminded us of our duty. I ordered another Coke, which I again drank slowly. At eleven o'clock, staff members returned and insisted that we leave. They went from trainee to trainee and physically walked each of us outside. Once we were all outside, they stood in the doorway until we wandered off. They were a distrustful bunch.

I walked slowly and unsteadily to my little van, parked a mile away, which would take me to my village. They crowded my fellow passengers and I in the back again, with no ventilation. I hoped that I would not feel the need to heave while in the back of the community bus.

When we finally reached a town, I realized that I still was not well, and I did not want anyone in the village I was visiting to see me in that condition. I left the van and found a small hotel to spend the night. I decided I would splurge—only five dollars for a room. I needed my privacy that night.

After dark, I felt hungry. I had not eaten anything during the last twenty-four hours. I found a little restaurant and ordered something light. As soon as I reached my room, I lost it all, but at least I lost it in the privacy of my room. After I recovered, I ordered a couple of Cokes so that I would have them during the night to settle my stomach. I tried to sleep. I found it better to sleep by stacking all the pillows and leaning against them in a near-sitting position. I cursed the rum that someone had put in the pineapple punch. I did not like pineapples anymore. In fact, I did not like anything or anybody.

I finished the last leg of my trip early the next morning. My first assignment was to find the man who had offered me my new place to live. With the help of people that I had met in the village, I found the wealthy, middle-aged farmer who had agreed to allow me to stay in one of his unused farmhouses. He would take me there at night and pick me up in the morning. I had the house to myself. It was a big house and in decent shape. He simply did not need it. Mostly, he stored stuff in it. Its location was perfect. It sat high on a hill with a view of the valley that contained the local town. The view was beautiful. The house had a wide porch on three sides. It was perfect for sitting and thinking. It had a running water, a working bathroom, and a cold-water shower. This house also would not meet the Peace Corps' specifications, but I did not know what else to do. I felt lucky that I had a place to stay.

The farmer took me to his house so that I could leave my little suitcase and so I could see where I would be staying. We spent ten minutes looking around. He was short, slightly overweight, and talked constantly. He was mostly bald, with the obligatory mustache. Already, the sun was hot, and there was no breeze. I could feel myself starting to sweat. The day would become uncomfortably warm if the breeze did not appear.

My Spanish was improving, but it was still lacking. Since I started with not knowing any Spanish, it would be a long way to being conversational in Spanish. I hoped my skill would improve this week.

October 10, 1967, Puerto Rico—Field Trip 3 and Return to Camp

I had been sitting on the porch of the house where I was staying, looking back over my last three field trips and the people that I had met. I think the ones who were the most patient with me while I was learning Spanish were those who could speak some English. They probably had the same difficulties learning English that I was having with Spanish, and so they empathized with my difficulties.

Yesterday I met a boy who was my age. He was finishing his work in the field. He and his father had three-quarters of an acre. He encouraged me in my endeavors to learn Spanish. Later in the afternoon, I walked farther up in the hills and talked with another family. They asked why I was in the area. I used my best Spanish to explain my mission to them. They were less than encouraging. I no longer remember exactly what they said, but I was ready to quit and return to the US after spending ten minutes with them. They were the definition of negativity.

I started to retrace my steps to my village when a boy and his father came out of the woods. I recognized them and addressed them by name. I usually did not remember names, but I remembered theirs. They were impressed, especially the father. He reached into a sack he was carrying and produced two of the largest, most beautiful oranges I had ever seen. He offered them to me. We conversed for ten minutes. He spoke slowly for me, and I understood much of what he said. Whenever he realized that I did not understand, he tried again using different words. He was patient and accepting, and through that, he was understanding and encouraging.

My view of the world changed completely. Within minutes, I went from talking with someone who was completely negative to talking with someone who was completely positive. They had recharged my batteries, and I was ready for more of whatever the world could throw at me.

The positive man made four dollars a day and had seven children. The cost of living here was not cheap. The value of land was high. An acre located on a steep slope could cost between $1,000 and $1,500. Their house was four hundred square feet. The entire family slept in one room. They lit each room with one forty-watt bulb each.

The next day, I was very tired because I had been helping to build a house. We poured concrete and dug out a driveway in preparation for concrete. We used pickaxes, shovels, and wheelbarrows to accomplish the task. I was happy that I was exhausted because I could not think, and I was tired of thinking—of worrying.

When I was working on the house the first day, I observed the other workers and duplicated their actions. I did not try to speak with them; they did not talk to me. They only used hand signals to communicate. The second day, I began to ask the proper word for each action; for example, mixing, watering down, and pouring. This naturally created short spurts of conversation. Still, some men would not communicate with me except with their hands; even so, I learned some useful new words.

October 12, 1967, Puerto Rico—Back in Camp, Classes Had Ceased

Everyone been packing for their departure. Classes had all but ceased. We had projects started and were trying to complete them. We finished a washhouse, which would accommodate three clothes washers and two dryers. The next group to train here would not need to grab a bucket and use a washboard to wash their clothes. We also began a new latrine, a recreation room, and a chicken house made from bamboo.

Friday night was the fiesta of all fiestas, or so they said. I had no intention of drinking anything beyond soda. I never wanted to drink pineapple punch again for the rest of my life. I would never again trust or drink any punch.

We trainees had mixed emotions. We were happy to be packing and preparing to move to the next stage of being a Peace Corps volunteer, but we were nervous about what awaited us in El Salvador. We continued to have the dropout problem. We were down to thirty-six people, as of that day, and we had no idea how many more were thinking about leaving. My two roommates from Philadelphia had both left, and that morning, one of my better friends also left. Deselection continued. It was difficult to anticipate who the ever-so-knowledgeable psychologist from New York City might judge unfit for duty. That brought the dropout rate for the El Salvador program to thirty-six percent. The Peace Corps told us that twenty-five percent was normal, but thirty-six percent was high.

The people who left the program early did so for varied reasons. Not being able to "take it" was often not the reason. Some trainees who left had excellent qualifications. One trainee already spoke fluent Spanish. A couple left because they decided they wanted to return to the USA and get married. Others decided that they would accept the jobs that a company had offered to them in the U.S. before they decided to join the Peace Corps.

We were all disappointed when one of our instructors left before the training was complete. He was a return Peace Corps volunteer from Colombia. The Peace Corps made a movie about him and the community in which he worked. His achievements were impressive. He was the Peace Corps volunteer that all trainees hoped they could become. He left to join the navy because the government wanted to draft him. He was very patriotic, but he did not believe in the war.

Last night, a twenty-two-year-old El Salvadorian teacher was trying to convince a trainee not to drop out of the program. The teacher only had a high school education from El Salvador and worked in community development there. The trainee, like me, spoke bad Spanish. The interesting thing to me was that the teacher understood the trainee's arguments perfectly, yet it could not have been from listening to the trainee's Spanish—none of us understood his Spanish. The teacher was marvelous at reading body language and other types of nonverbal communication. The Peace Corps did an excellent job at selecting the best people to teach us. In the end, the trainee left the program.

The El Salvadorian Peace Corps director arrived. She updated us on where they would station each volunteer in El Salvador. They informed us that most of us would have electricity, but refrigerators and other luxuries would be available to only a few of us.

Among the diverse trainee professions, one was a registered nurse. Unlike the rest of us, she already had received her assignment. She was to work in a hospital in San Salvador, where she would begin without being assigned to any specific floor. Later, they would assign her to a floor when the hospital was able to select a head nurse for that floor. The problem was that the hospital had to find a head nurse who would accept change and actively collaborate with the volunteer to achieve it. The goal was to make that hospital floor a model for nursing in El Salvador. At the end of our nurse's two-year term, they hoped that her floor would be operating efficiently and could be used to train other nurses.

October 16, 1967, Deselection is Completed

The psychologist and the camp director completed the deselection process. I made it. I passed my conversational Spanish test with a minimal passing grade. They rated us on a five-point scale. The scale reserved a five for college-educated native speakers. A few Americans could obtain a 4+, but no nonnative achieved a five. I obtained a 1+, the minimum required to become a volunteer. That score was not impressive, but it was not easy for me to obtain. *Survival precedes excellence*—that was my motto, and I survived!

October 17, 1967, Flight to San Salvador

We packed for our journey to San Salvador. There was little to pack because we had almost nothing. The buses arrived, and we loaded our suitcases. We said goodbye to the camp and headed back to San Juan.

When they called our flight, we entered the plane and settled in. When the flight attendant closed the door on the airplane, I knew that when it opened, I would be in Central America, in San Salvador. I would be in the country that we had studied in sixth grade. As a student, I tried to imagine what these countries were like. I would know very soon. I was ecstatically happy and frightfully scared.

For me, the flight attendant's act of closing now and later opening the plane's door represented the ending of one chapter in my life and the opening of another. The flight itself was a surreal experience of dreams about what had just happened and what was about to happen. I felt like a rodeo clown who had jumped into his protective barrel. He could be glad to be alive but reluctant to stick his head out. He had to remain mindful that the bull could hit the barrel at any time, yet he knew he had to stick his head out eventually.

Chapter 3

My Journey in El Salvador Begins

October 28, 1967—Off to El Salvador

Everyone was on the plane from San Juan except one volunteer; he was sick and would remain in San Juan until the doctors resolved his health problems.

After a two-hour flight, we landed in Guatemala City, where we were surprised by how chilly it was, given that we were in the tropics. We never realized that Guatemala City was a mile high. We made a quick dash around the airport to warm up. We had thirty minutes before we had to board the plane again for the last leg of our flight.

We took off and landed twenty minutes later in San Salvador. The plane climbed only for ten minutes before it started its descent, demonstrating how small the Central American countries were. As we circled San Salvador for our final approach, I saw the reflection of the moon in Lake Ilopango (e-low-*pan*-go), a lake formed in the crater of an extinct volcano.

We left the plane and descended to the tarmac and walked toward the airport. There was no band playing, just us volunteers walking into the unknown. Then, from a dark second-story balcony, cheering and clapping broke out. We struggled to see where it was coming from. It was current Peace Corps volunteers who had made the trip to San Salvador to welcome us. I learned later that they were there to view the new volunteers to be the first to stake their claims on someone they fancied. No one staked a claim on me. I could only surmise that I was too young for the much-older female volunteers. I was twenty years old; they were twenty-three to twenty-eight years old.

As soon as we entered the airport, two photographers appeared and took a group photograph. The photograph appeared in the next day's newspaper. We then went to our *pensión* (pen-see-*own*), Latin America's equivalent of a motel. By US standards, it was not much, but by Peace Corps standards, it was just dandy. Surprise—a party spontaneously broke out. Someone had found a roaming band of musicians who were happy to serenade us for a small fee.

That finished our eventful day. I retreated to my bed and prepared to sleep, but I could not sleep. I was too excited. I was in El Salvador. I *really* was in El Salvador, the same country that I studied in the sixth grade. Now I could add to the photographs I had already seen in our encyclopedia, the street noises I heard from my bed, and the scents reaching my nose. I pulled the sheet around my body and smiled to myself. My great adventure had started.

The next morning, a Peace Corps staff member appeared early at our pensión to tell us that we needed to be in the Peace Corps office by nine o'clock. The staff member left the address for us with brief directions. I had no idea where to go. I knew it was too far to walk and too expensive by taxi. We needed to go by bus, but which bus or buses? My strategy was to find the volunteer who spoke the best Spanish and attach myself to him until we arrived at the office.

We spent the next three days filling out more forms and listening to speeches and then more speeches. The U.S. Ambassador invited us to a party at the U.S. ambassador's house for our first night in-country. I did not feel comfortable because we were supposed to dress up. I was insecure because there were so many high-level dignitaries present. As a Nebraska farm boy, I never saw myself shaking hands with a US ambassador. There were fewer than two hundred American ambassadors in the world, and I was about to meet one of them.

Having arrived at the party, I hung back in a corner and watched while the other volunteers spoke comfortably to the ambassador and his children, whose ages were from teens to twenty. I wondered what their life must be like from day to day. There also were dignitaries present. All my colleagues moved about smoothly from one person to another, with a drink in their hands and a smile on their faces. I had no drink and only a forced smile. I was not happy. I was in the shadows, nervous, and I looked at my watch constantly. I was out of my comfort zone, and I did not like it. I kept an eye open for any other volunteer who showed signs of thinking about leaving. I would volunteer to go with him or her. Escape was my only thought.

The next day, we received our permanent assignments. This was a huge moment. They were sending me to the city of Sonsonate (sown-so- *nah*-tay), which was in the northwest corner of El Salvador, close to Guatemala. The city was located eight miles from the ocean, less than two hours by bus from San Salvador. It had about forty thousand inhabitants. At first, I was disappointed. The image I had of being a Peace Corps volunteer was to live far from civilization in a small village, without electricity or other amenities. But no, where I was going, all kinds of fruit, vegetables, meat, dairy products, and coconuts were available. Electricity and running water were available. It even had three movie theaters, although not of the same quality as in the USA. The city even had its own bus system and soccer team.

I would not be roughing it; however, it would be nice to occasionally see a movie or to eat ice cream. The downside to all this luxury was that Sonsonate was located on the flat plains and was hot, hot, hot.

October 29, 1967—My First Trip to Sonsonate and Nahuizalco

My assignment was to find my way from San Salvador to the Indian village of Nahuizalco (nah-we-*zal*-co). First, I needed to cross the city from the *pensión* to the bus station. Second, I had to travel from San Salvador's bus station to Sonsonate's bus station. Third, once in Sonsonate, I needed to find and take the next bus to Nahuizalco, a village five miles northeast of Sonsonate. There, I would meet my Peace Corps volunteer mentors, Bob and Shirley, a married couple who had resided there for one year.

My first task was to take a city bus from my *pensión* in San Salvador to the intercity bus station, which was located across town. I do not remember how I did it, but I did it. Then, I found a bus that would take me to Sonsonate. I did it, but there was a problem. Unbeknownst to me, there were three types of intercity bus services in El Salvador. First, there were direct buses. These buses left San Salvador and did not stop until they arrived at the destination. It cost more, but the trip was fast and direct. My bus was not this type.

The second type was a bus that went from point A to point B but made several stops in smaller cities and towns located on or close to the highway along the way. These villages were located two or three miles away from the main highway. Once the bus reached each of these stops, it unloaded people and merchandise before loading new passengers and merchandise. This process could take ten to twenty minutes, and they made a half dozen of these stops along the way. A trip on this type of bus cost less than the first type of bus, but it could take twice as long as the direct bus. My bus was not this type of bus either.

The third type of bus not only stopped in the towns along the way but also stopped to pick up and unload passengers along the highway. Whenever anyone wanted off the bus, the driver stopped the bus and unloaded a passenger and his or her merchandise. Whenever a person stepped out from a coffee plantation and waved at the driver, the driver stopped the bus. The passenger boarded and they loaded his or her merchandise. Seldom did the bus travel more than one mile without stopping to drop off passengers and merchandise or to pick up others. This was the type of bus I was riding. Because I had been unaware of the three types of bus service, the fifty-five-mile trip to Sonsonate was unbearably long and confusing.

I only had an idea where Sonsonate was located. Each time we took a turn off the main highway, I thought I had caught the wrong bus. When this happened, I caught the attention of the ticket-taker and asked if this bus was going to Sonsonate. He always answered yes, and then we turned and went somewhere that was not Sonsonate. If I had understood about the different bus services, my trip would have been much less stressful.

Eventually, I saw a highway sign indicating that Sonsonate was fifteen miles ahead. My anxiety decreased, and I relaxed. All I had to do was to stay with the bus until it stopped at the bus station, and I would have successfully reached my second destination.

As soon as the bus stopped at the station, I waited for the bus assistants to drop my suitcase from the top of the bus. When I had my bag, I looked for a ticket window to buy passage to Nahuizalco. I thought I had found it at the front of a lengthy line. I wished I could have been sure. I wanted to go to the front of the line and ask if they sold tickets to Nahuizalco, but that would mean delaying everyone else who was standing in line behind me. This would have been especially annoying to the well-mannered

Indians waiting patiently in line. I thought that the better option would be to wait in line like everyone else.

Slowly, the line advanced. Once I was in front of the ticket seller, I tried to ask for a ticket to Nahuizalco. I had been rehearsing what I would say since I entered the line. He told me that I was in the wrong line and that I needed to go to another line, but I was not sure. To avoid delaying the locals, I left the line and started to look around like I knew what I was doing. I walked a few feet and detained a bus driver. I asked him where I could buy a ticket to Nahuizalco. He pointed to another line ten yards around the corner. I went there, waited in another extensive line, and then bought my ticket.

I had to wait two hours for my bus to leave. I tried to be inconspicuous and leaned against a wall at the entrance to the bus station. Yes, right! I was six feet tall, and everyone else was five feet tall and change. I was white, and they were not. I tried to look like I was in my environment. I was not. I kept looking at my watch. No one else had a watch, and they already knew the time, at least close enough to meet their needs. I wondered what Nahuizalco would look like and wished I were already there.

Finally, I saw a bus come in with its sign indicating that it had come from Nahuizalco. I followed it and gave it time to unload. I asked the driver if it was my bus. It was. I climbed aboard. Within a half hour, we crept out of the bus station and started crossing Sonsonate. It was my first look at the city. It was a busy city. People were everywhere. There were so many people in the streets that one person could not move without bumping into another person, and each car, truck, and ox cart risked running over people every time it moved.

As we reached the edge of the far side of the city, the paved road turned into a well-maintained dirt road. We started a slow ascent into the foothills that would take us to Nahuizalco. After thirty minutes, we entered what I assumed was Nahuizalco. I was not sure because there were no road signs. The bus went to the town square and parked. I optimistically grabbed my bag, boldly stepped out of the bus, and looked around, thinking, *I am in the middle of an Indian village in rural El Salvador. What am I doing?*

I dug out directions to Bob and Shirley's house, written on a small, crumpled paper, from my pants pocket. I had to walk a couple of blocks ahead, turn, and go in another direction. Their house was the third house on the left on that block. I picked what I thought was the third house and knocked. It was their house, and they spoke English. I was happy. After only a half day on my own, I already missed speaking English.

They invited me into their home. They were as curious about me as I was about them. They lived in a large, old, and poorly maintained house. It had one large empty room: a living room located next to the front door. The rest of the house was located around a central open area with dirt in its center. It had enough space to make a nice garden. On one side of the patio were a bedroom and a smaller room used as a study. On the other side were a kitchen and another room that they used for storage. They paid sixteen dollars a month rent. They put me in the storage room. I did not mind; I was simply happy to be someplace.

October 30, 1967, Nahuizalco—Monday

Shirley was an excellent cook. She baked in an oven that she had created. She had found a bulk biscuit tin that was as large as a four- gallon rectangular container. She removed one end and reattached it by poking holes in the top and used a wire to function as a hinge. She placed the four-gallon container on a gas burner, and—presto—she had a small oven. It was basic, but it worked.

After we ate, Shirley took us into the rural area—the *campo*. The early afternoon was no longer cool. We would be sweating soon. It was comforting being with someone who was known locally by the people. People spent less time staring at me. Everyone we met smiled and bid a good morning to Shirley. The women knew Shirley well. They looked at Bob and me and said nothing, although some men nodded at him. Shirley wore a sunbonnet and carried a big, locally made bag on her arm. In this, she had the items she needed for the day's lesson with the local ladies. Her walk was fast and determined. She was a lady on a mission.

The cobblestone street lies in front of the house. After walking a couple of blocks, the cobblestone turned to dirt, and the path narrowed. Brush and trees rimmed each side of the path. The road became one lane, which was wide enough for most purposes. If one truck met another truck, one could pull over and allow the other to maneuver around it. Cars, trucks, and oxcarts moved in both directions and managed to pass each other when they met.

The soil was black, clearly of volcanic origin. I knew this because I had had a course in soil science. In the background was the most beautiful and perfectly formed volcano I had ever seen. It was gorgeous; it had no vegetation on it. Later, I learned that it had last erupted in January 1932. They called the volcano Izalco (e-*zal*-co). There was also a town nearby that they called Izalco, another Indian village.

After walking more than a half mile, I saw a large building complex that contained an area larger than six football fields. I asked Shirley what it was. She said that it was a coffee *beneficio*, a place where they collected coffee, like a grain elevator, and they dried it by manually spreading it thinly on an adobe floor. When the sun was out, men with homemade rakes walked back and forth to stir the beans and facilitate the natural drying. The beneficio employed dozens of people during the coffee-picking season.

Upon reaching the *beneficio*, the road split, and we took the left branch, which now was only a path. On the path we chose, the women carried things on their heads, and the men carried loads in their arms or on their backs. The path descended quickly. Below, I saw two streams merging into one stream. On the other side of the streams, I saw a path zigzagging up a steep hill. I tried to visualize what lay in front of us. After two dozen steps more, I saw a hammock bridge crossing the single stream. As we approached the bridge, I saw that it was far above the stream, and it consisted of four boards for walking. It had flimsy handrails to catch any poor souls who lost their balance. The base often had one board missing, and the rails also had many missing segments. It was not reassuring. For anyone who took a misstep, the fall was far, and the landing would be painful.

Shirley went first. After she crossed, Bob started. Bob had waited for Shirley to completely cross before he started, but I started after Bob had taken a dozen steps. The bridge was long. I understood immediately why Bob had waited. When a person stepped onto the unbraced bridge, it began to undulate, thus making waves. When one person was walking, it was not a problem. When two or more people were walking on the bridge, each person created his or her own waves. Sometimes the waves canceled each other, and sometimes they reinforced each other, making the waves more pronounced. The problem was that the people crossing the bridge thought they knew where the planks would be when they set down their feet, but they did not. The bridge planks were always moving. Sometimes the planks were closer than they thought, and their feet would catch the planks and cause them to fall forward.

Stumbling on this bridge was never good. Sometimes the planks were farther from their feet than they thought, and they again fell forward. I imagined that such misjudged steps could have been the cause of the missing side rails, or it was due to the many Indian men crossing the bridge in an inebriated state which caused them to fall against the side rails. That could explain why the rails were missing.

With the image of the broken side rails in mind, I started to walk slowly, placing each foot firmly on the bridge floor before raising the other. Then a new problem occurred. Indian people on the path started to cross the bridge at two or three times my speed. They were comfortable with the bridge's wave motions and were comfortably walking much faster than I was. They created new undulations that confused my feet. I had to move over to open the passing lane to allow them to pass me. That pressed me against the side rail—if there was a side rail. I felt like the hammock bridge was going to spin around like hammocks with sleeping people often did. I was a nervous wreck.

Shirley did not wait for us. She knew we would catch up eventually. Bob waited for me because Bob liked conversation, especially in English. Bob and I climbed the steep slope up the hill. As we climbed, Bob gave me a history of the region.

The path up the slope had suffered water erosion over the decades and had uncovered rocks and hard substrate. Thousands of Indians' feet passed over the substrate's edges, wearing them smooth, while others were still sharp. I noticed that nearly all the Indians treading the path were barefoot. The bottoms of their feet had to be as tough as leather to withstand the sharpness of the substrate's edges.

The climb up the rocky path was about the length of two football fields. When we reached the top, I was breathing heavily. I looked out at the landscape from the plateau that we had just reached. I saw excellent farmland. When I looked up, the volcano Izalco appeared so close that I could reach out and touch it. I could easily see long distances with clarity because the air was pure and unpolluted.

Bob and I visited three or four family homes in the area. The peasants made the roofs from tall grass which they collected. They made their walls from homemade bricks, and the floors of dirt. The furnishings inside were equally meager. They made their bed frames from midsize tree branches that they had worked with basic wood tools into four-by-four pieces. The mattress consisted of homemade rope laced across the wooden bedframe in both directions and covered with a homemade mat, made from the edges of the reed locally called *tule* (*too*-lay).

Tule was a plant that needed an abundance of water to grow. The women harvested it and then fashioned it into mats that they used on beds to soften the sharpness of the rope lattice. The also used mats on floors to sit on or even to make baskets, hats, and a host of other products. They made everything used in building their homes and furniture. They even made the clay pots they used to cook on a wood fire. Little that these Indians did was registered in the nation's gross domestic product.

After spending one day with Bob and Shirley, I made a few observations about their approach to Peace Corps work. Shirley worked with the Indian women in the *cantones* (can-*toe*-nays)—a small, rural geographical/political area. Her goal was to improve the Indian families' nutrition and health. Shirley was a doer. Bob tried to collaborate with the men, but mostly he philosophized with them and asked questions about their history in that region. He was interested in culture, anthropology, and religion. Bob was a dreamer.

November 3, 1967, Nahuizalco—Living with Shirley and Bob

I received my first mail outside of San Salvador. This was different from our Puerto Rico camp, where we received mail twice a day. I would receive my mail once a week, at least until I received my new permanent address, which would be in a couple of weeks.

Bob continued to introduce me to his acquaintances in the *cantón* Pushtan. Shirley had meetings and was always giving classes to the *campesinas* (kam-pay-*see*-nas), or Indian ladies. Bob talked and philosophized. Shirley no longer accompanied us. She was dynamic and was always busy. Shirley did not do slow walking. She only had one gear: high. Bob was more laid-back and flexible. The walking was constant and was tiresome. It was all up and down hills, on narrow, uneven paths and through fields. Bob did not always want to go far. He preferred staying in the *cantones* that were close to Nahuizalco.

Today, Bob and I went to two *cantones*. Each *cantón* consisted of a small aggregation of homes, but dozens of people lived there. People were everywhere. El Salvador's high population density was obvious in rural areas and impacted me in unusual ways. The good old days of taking a half dozen steps off the path to have a tinkle was history. There were so many people in rural El Salvador that when you thought you were alone, you were not. You were never alone. Someone was watching you from behind a coffee tree or a clump of grass. Let the one who tinkles in fresh air beware!

Bob introduced me to an Indian leader and progressive farmer. He rented an area measured in *tareas* (ta-ray-as). One *tarea* equaled 625 square yards, or an area represented by twenty-five yards by twenty-five yards, or one-eighth of an acre. With it, he fed himself and his family. He had six children still alive. When we asked the Indians how many children they had, they responded by giving the total number of children they had had and how many were still alive. The proportion was usually about one half. It was common for the women to have ten or twelve children, with only five or six surviving.

I met another progressive Indian farmer through Bob. Bob knew everyone. The farmer had taken part in corn demonstrations for three years. Last year, he came in first place out of thirty demonstrations. Before he could harvest his corn that year, someone did it for him by stealing his corn production. Since the campesino rented land, and he could not pay the rent, the land own took the land from him for the next year for nonpayment of rent. In this region, renting land was difficult. Losing a plot of rented land was a catastrophe for a farmer. Now, he had no land to farm, no money from last year's crop, and no landowner who would rent to him for next year. He was in a difficult position, and all because of the greedy, dishonest person who had stolen his crop.

Bob, out of kindness, hired this farmer to haul dirt into his small patio garden. The existing soil was poor, so Bob hired the farmer to cart in better soil from outside of town with an oxcart. This was not an ideal or permanent solution for the ex-farmer, but Bob helped the man out of a tough situation. That explained why, as harvest approached, farmers slept in their fields. It was a tough existence that resulted in farmers harvesting crops before they reached the perfect point of ripeness, but if the farmers waited until the crop was ripe, thieves could steal the entire crop.

American farmers described their land in hundreds or thousands of acres. One acre consists of seven to eight *tareas*. In this region, the farmer with one acre of land to farm was a fortunate farmer; most had far less.

In my walks around the rural area with Bob, I saw two types of temporary dams constructed by the Indians. The small farmers could not depend on the government for any help. The government had always seen the Indians as an embarrassment to the country, at best; and at worst, the government sought ways to annihilate them, as they did to thousands of peasants in the 1932 Massacre—a story for another time.

The first type of temporary dam involved piling large rocks by hand. They stopped piling them when the water rose high enough behind the rocks to serve their purpose. This style dam allowed water to pass through so that farmers below the dam would not be denied water. The disadvantage was that the Indians had to reconstruct it after each heavy rain, but the Indians had been doing this for centuries.

A second type of temporary dam that Indians built was by laying a coconut tree trunk across the stream. They tied tree branches, two to three feet long and three to five inches in diameter, to the coconut tree trunk. They piled rocks and dirt behind the tree branches to keep them in place. The water would rise and flow over the boards. These dams were ingenious and required no money—and no government involvement. The Indians were very independent. They had to be to have survived for so many centuries in a hostile environment.

Bob introduced me as an irrigation specialist to a small farmer, who jumped up and down with excitement and dragged Bob and me to his little orchard. He showed us his oranges, which were splitting and rotting on the tree. Some of his trees were even dying. His work foreman thought that it was due to the new moon. I suggested that I take samples of his oranges to El Salvador's agricultural college, located in Santa Tecla, a small city this side of San Salvador. The farmer found a bag, and we picked four split oranges and placed them into the bag.

The next day, I went to Santa Tecla and found the citrus specialist. He examined the oranges and informed me that the cause was a copper deficiency; plus, there was insect damage. Now I had to convince the landowner that the moon was not the cause of this affliction. The real problem was that the man in charge of doing the work believed that the moon was causing the problem and was not likely to follow any directions given to him.

I wished I knew how to resolve the problem, but I did not. I heard that we had an agricultural extension agent in Sonsonate who might have a solution. I would find him as soon as I returned to Sonsonate.

As we walked around the Nahuizalco area, we continually met people. Bob always stopped them and introduced me to them as an agronomist and irrigation specialist, but that made me uncomfortable. I had completed two years in the College of Agriculture, but that did not make me either an agronomist or a specialist in irrigation. I had worked ten years irrigating crops on our family farm, but that was a special situation, one not likely to duplicate itself in El Salvador. I asked him to stop.

November 5, 1967, Nahuizalco—Religious Indians

Today I learned that the Indians were religious—very Catholic, but their style of Catholicism was unusual. They superimposed their old Indian religions on Catholicism. This blending occurred when the Spanish were killing Indians who did not convert to Catholicism. The Indians were not stupid. They outwardly converted, but inwardly, they remained true to their own gods. Instead of openly worshiping their Indian gods, they found saints with similar characteristics as their gods and began paying homage to those saints, as stand-ins for their gods. Priests often suspected that this was occurring, but they could do nothing about it because the Indians were doing what the Spanish demanded— worshiping the Catholic way, in their own way.

November 6, 1967, Nahuizalco—I Visit the Agricultural Extension Office

I took the bus from Nahuizalco to Sonsonate and discovered the location of the Agricultural Extension Office. I found the office and introduced myself to the four-member staff: Vicente (ve-*sin*-tay), the agronomist; América, the home economist; Myra (*Me*-rah), the happy secretary; and a janitor/messenger (I cannot remember his name).

Vicente was twenty-seven to thirty years old. He always wore clothes that would allow him to make a sudden visit to the rural area, or travel to Santa Tecla for a meeting with his superiors without feeling overdressed or underdressed. He wore a cowboy hat because it made sense in a sunny and hot environment. He impressed me as being technically competent.

América was fortyish, divorced, with two children between eight and twelve years old. It was difficult to read her age. Her face was beginning to wrinkle. Her clothes were homemade, with stiches that were not close together. This made me believe she was busy and had not had an easy life. América was friendly, while Vicente was indifferent.

Myra also was around twenty-seven to thirty years old, plump, with a round face that always had a smile on it. She knew everything that was worth knowing in the city and would never turn down the opportunity to learn more. She was married to a trucker who owned a large eighteen-wheeler Volvo, in which he hauled material around El Salvador. Myra would not allow her husband to truck outside of El Salvador. She insisted that he be home with her each night. She kept him on a short leash. I sensed that, should he ever misbehave, she would hand down a harsh punishment. He was afraid of her and always behaved himself.

The janitor was seventy to seventy-five years old. He was thin and very humble; he wore small spectacles and walked slowly and bent over. He was friendly, but as soon as we finished shaking hands and introducing ourselves, he withdrew to observe from a distance. He seemed accustomed to being in the background.

After explaining who I was and what I wanted, which was no small task, given my limited Spanish, Vicente explained to me how the farmer should combat his copper deficiency and insect problem. He conveyed the solution precisely and then disengaged. América, however, had listened intently to Vicente's solution, and when he left the conversation, she swooped in to keep it going. She was very friendly— mother-like.

I explained that I would be doing literacy work with peasants in another agency and that I needed to find a place to stay for the next two years. I told América that I had no idea how to do this. She grabbed my hand and led me toward the door. She yelled back at Myra that she would be out for a while.

We left the office, and she took the lead, walking. I hurried to keep up. I noticed América's bulging calf muscles—muscles not acquired from casual strolls. I could see that she had logged many miles, walking.

The sidewalks were very narrow, often allowing only one person on them at a time. To avoid walking in the street, I fell behind her in single file, but I had to hurry to avoid losing sight of her. Finally, we had to walk in the street and around the slow-moving oxcarts. We had to watch out for cars, trucks, and buses. We also had to watch out for other people in the street, most of whom were carrying something to or from the local market. The streets were more than crowded; they were a sea of humanity. Sometimes, it was difficult to know that we were walking in a street. All I could see were people's heads, bobbing up and down. Only when a vehicle approached did I see the people run for the sides, opening a narrow strip in the street for the vehicle to pass.

After walking a couple of miles at a brisk pace, I was panting. América was not. We had entered the central business district, crossed the central business district, left it behind, and entered the outskirts on the other side of town. These outskirts were nothing like a city's outskirts in the US. The street was paved but narrow. The traffic was two-way, but vehicles could only travel one way safely at a time. Anytime vehicles met, the outcome always was in doubt if one vehicle did not pull over and wait for the other to pass.

The sidewalks were no more than a yard wide and sometimes only a foot wide. The street side of the houses was all plaster-covered adobe. Each house shared an interior wall with their neighbor. Most houses were from ten to twenty-five feet wide and very deep, often going back more than one hundred feet from the front door.

Suddenly, América turned and faced a doorway. She was smiling and asked permission to enter the house. The room was approximately twenty by fifteen feet and used as a *tienda*—a small commercial enterprise located in residential areas that sold life's essentials. Today, they would be called a Latin-style convenience store.

América walked toward a woman who was around thirty-five years old, full-bodied, and smiling. América and she exchanged greetings, along with small talk, but the woman was distracted. She talked to América but looked at me. She waited for America to get to the point. She was excited because she knew the reason for her visit involved me. Americans were a novelty in this part of the world. Everyone wanted to know an American.

América introduced me to Doña Maria and then explained my situation. Doña Maria nodded understandingly. The first question she asked me was if I was a Mormon missionary. I explained to her that I was a Peace Corps volunteer. I saw by her facial expression that she did not understand the distinction.

She signaled for us to follow her. She turned to take us through the back door from the *tienda* into a covered patio, used as a dining hall for her renters. There was a long open patio used to hang washed clothes on one side; on the other side were three rooms that she rented. Each room was about eight by twelve feet, with a wooden window and a wooden door; both opened from the middle and had slates for ventilation. At the back end of the open patio were three compartments: the bathroom, which contained a flush toilet and cold-water shower; a covered area, which the maid used to wash clothes; and a small area enclosed by bamboo slats, used by the maid as her tiny sleeping quarters. This area had no door or windows.

Doña Maria explained how much I would pay to rent the room, eat all meals, and have my clothes washed. It fit my budget, so I rented the room. I felt relieved. This solved my major problem. My life in Sonsonate was going to be easy. I had a flush toilet and running water and someone to cook and serve my meals and to wash and iron my clothes. I would be the envy of most Peace Corps volunteers. And América had made it possible, an act of kindness that I would always remember. I would move in four days later on Saturday, November 11, 1968.

November 11, 1967, Sonsonate—I Move into My Room

The day I moved in, I took a bus from Nahuizalco to Sonsonate and walked the couple of miles from the bus station to my new room. I kept consulting the paper in my hand for the house number while I watched for the same number on the street. Most house fronts looked the same. I had only been to the house once, and I could not remember its exact location.

As I walked along the street, I attracted attention. People stopped to watch me walk by. This made me uncomfortable.

I found the house number that matched that on my paper and meekly entered the open door. There was Doña Maria, attending to customers at her worn counter. She smiled and left her customers, walked around her counter, and ushered me back to my room. I felt better. I left my travel bag in my room and returned with Doña Maria to her *tienda*. She finished dispatching her customers and turned her full attention to me.

I needed a bed. Doña Maria suggested a scissor bed. It was simple and inexpensive. I liked the inexpensive part. She said that if I gave her the money, she could send the maid's boyfriend to buy the cot and transport it back to my room. I gave her the money. She also asked if I would permit the maid to take an old chair into my room. I did. I kept my clothes in a suitcase. My only furniture consisted of my cot and her chair. My room was simple.

A scissor bed was like an army cot but with a few differences. A scissor bed was bigger. It was twice as wide and twice as far off the floor as an army cot. The scissor legs were much stronger. They made them from wood that was more than three by three inches. The ends of the cot did not have wooden cross supports; this was good and bad. At the head end, I wanted the cross board to provide better support for my head, but at my foot end, I enjoyed being able to dangle my feet over the soft end, rather than the wooden brace on an army cot.

The maid and her boyfriend were wonderful people. They both worked long hours but made little in wages. The boyfriend worked at the railroad. He was a machinist or something similar. He and dozens of other men kept the trains' steam engines running. These were engines from the nineteenth century, from before Butch Cassidy and the Sundance Kid. I did not know where the boyfriend lived, but Doña Maria allowed him to stay in the small room with the maid as often as they wanted. In return, he ran errands for Doña Maria. El Salvador had a huge hidden economy where people without money did each other favors.

In El Salvador, many stores stayed open late; at least they stayed open past six in the evening. I had my hair cut at six; the barber finished at seven. In his defense, he was thorough. He had another customer waiting when I left. It cost me twenty cents. I offered no complaints and no tip.

After having my hair cut, I stopped in a small sidewalk restaurant for a snack before walking home. The girl who waited on me was between sixteen and eighteen years old. Her shift had started at 7:00

a.m. and finished at 8:30 p.m. She worked seven days a week. The number of hours worked per week was at least ninety. She received no overtime pay.

After eating, I slowly walked from downtown to my room. I had a better idea where it was now. It was dark as I walked up the street toward my house. When I crossed the railroad tracks, I knew that I was almost home. Approaching my house, the streetlights lit the streets well, and I could see people and children sitting on their steps by their front doors, while other children rushed about playing under their parents' watchful eyes. I was nervous and did not want to parade myself in front of so many people, but I had no choice. I had to walk the gauntlet. As I passed the steps of each house, I gave my best *buenas noches* and moved on to the next house, only a step or two farther up the street, to give my evening greeting, repeatedly. I could feel people's eyes following my every step and felt their talking accelerate after I turned into the *tienda*.

I gave another *buenas noches* to Doña Maria and retreated through the patio, entered my room, closed the door, and lay on my bed. The day had exhausted me, and I was ready to sleep.

November 12, 1967, Sonsonate—Our Portable Libraries

I was bored all day. I understood why the instructor in camp told us to be prepared for boredom. It was something that plagued all Peace Corps volunteers. We had to use it to our advantage. To help us, the Peace Corps made a deal with book publishers and purchased thousands of copies of books that the Peace Corps distributed to its volunteers. They placed about one hundred books in each volunteer's library. A two-shelved cardboard bookcase held the library. The objective was to give volunteers something to do during their less-active times. I thought it was considerate and ingenuous of the Peace Corps. I read more books during my time in the Peace Corps than I did during any other two-year period in my life.

One of my friends was in an isolated village, high in the mountains. His town had no electricity, no market, no library, nothing outside of one bar, which had a generator to power a light bulb and a beer cooler from 6:00 to 8:00 p.m. These cardboard libraries were useful for him— during the day. They were useful to me during the rainy season, when we could not travel to the rural areas.

Within a couple of weeks, the Peace Corps would place another volunteer in Sonsonate. That would make it easier for both of us. I thought that we could do things together on weekends, and we would have someone to talk with in English when we became frustrated. I was looking forward to seeing him.

While I was out walking, I ran into four Latter-Day Saints missionaries, who were my age. I understood why most people I met thought that I was a missionary; I did not realize that Sonsonate had four missionaries.

Subsequently, I learned that much of the Sonsonate population did not think well of missionaries. The people believed they had the right to practice religion without missionaries trying to convince them to change to another religion. They did not want to debate religion. I did not want to spend too much time with them, for fear that people would associate me with missionaries. I represented the Peace Corps, and I wanted that to become better known.

Later that same day, I discovered that two teenage girls lived immediately across from my house. They were both juniors in high school. Celia attended a Catholic school in San Salvador. She returned to see her family on vacations and special weekends. Celia's father was a small rancher. He had about 160 acres. Her mother operated a brick factory out of her large backyard. They were economically better off than the other teen's parents. Maria studied locally. Maria's parents were both teachers. Since teachers earned little income, they needed to live frugally. Celia and Maria had known each other all their lives and were excellent friends.

I enjoyed talking with Celia and Maria; it helped me to improve my Spanish, and they were kind, intelligent, and funny. We often sat on their front steps and talked the evening away. I was in heaven because I had always had difficulties starting and maintaining conversations with ladies. In my first two years at the university, I had never had a date; in fact, I seldom even spoke with any female outside of class. I was a social misfit, but in El Salvador, I lost my inhibitions and found that these young ladies were interested in me, at first because I was an American, but later, we simply enjoyed each other's company.

Everyone in the neighborhood sat on their front steps at night to talk. Parents sat with each other or with their children. It was a very sociable environment. While the girls and I talked on their steps, I had to be careful not to fully extend my legs onto the narrow sidewalk, or I risked a vehicle driving over them. Vehicles passed by within a couple of feet of the house's front door.

Maria's mother, Doña Juana, liked me and talked to me as she ironed clothes. She was a busy woman. I do not remember ever seeing her at rest. She took a bus to the market and returned with her purchases in bags, carried by her tired hands. She cooked food without the benefit of frozen or instant food. Sonsonate had a population between 40,000 and 45,000 and did not have one fast-food restaurant, nor did markets sell food that could be quickly prepared. Doña Juana had to clean the house, wash clothes by hand, and iron all clothes, because nothing was permanent press. And she taught school full time.

Even with her busy schedule, she allowed me to ramble on about silly things. I persuaded her to correct my Spanish when I made huge mistakes, and each day my Spanish improved. If she had corrected all my numerous mistakes, I doubt that we could have had a conversation.

She became a pseudo-mother for me, but Maria's father was different. He and the other men of the neighborhood were more distant. They were friendly, but I knew that they did not like me or trust me. I was young and naïve, and I was not sharp at reading people's thoughts. Being from Nebraska, I always trusted people and believed in them, at least until they lied to me.

I also was becoming attached to Doña Maria, my landlady. She cooked wonderful meals for me. They were simple and economical but delicious. I especially started to look forward to my evening meal. Occasionally, she would prepare a small piece of meat, rice with a soft egg on top, and fried plantains with extra-thick cream on top. It was a meal I would remember.

I developed a routine. After my evening meal, I grabbed a kitchen chair and placed it next to the wall of her *tienda*. I opened my Spanish book to a random page and studied whatever the topic was. Sometimes, when her customers entered to make a purchase, my eyes were in the book, but I analyzed every word they spoke. Every day I picked up a word or two, or

I learned a new way to say something with words I already knew. When the customer left, I continued skimming the book for grammar ideas. My goal was to learn one new thing every day and then employ it the next day. And I did. Day by day, my Spanish improved.

November 16, 1967, Sonsonate—I Met a Veterinarian

In the Agricultural Extension Office, where I spent much of my time, I had the pleasure of meeting one of the veterinarians who rented a room next to mine. Our schedules were different, so I seldom saw him, but once when our paths crossed, I asked him to take me to the ranches he visited so that I could form a better picture of the livestock-production system. He agreed and helped me with my Spanish. He was married and lived in San Salvador. He had three daughters, ages three, fourteen, and sixteen. They could not speak a word of English, but he claimed they wanted to learn.

November 23, 1967, San Salvador—Thanksgiving Day

I went to Santa Tecla with a *campesino* (cam-pay-*see*-no)—a farm peasant—to obtain information about a fishpond. Unfortunately, I learned nothing. I was disappointed I had made the sacrifice of traveling so far to learn something but did not learn anything. Since it was only ten in the morning, the campesino and I separated; he went his way, and I proceeded to San Salvador to visit the Peace Corps office. I wanted to see if I had received any mail because I missed my family.

Bingo! I had received eight letters. I was happy, especially since this was my first Thanksgiving Day away from the family. I was feeling low, and these letters helped improve my mood. The Peace Corps subdirector stopped by the office and invited me to his place for dinner. That was kind of him. We had fried chicken, mashed potatoes, fresh vegetables, and fresh cookies. It was all prepared by his cook, who knew how to prepare American food. I was happy, although still lonely.

My trunk arrived, and it could not have come at a better time. I had to return to San Salvador the next day for eight days of meetings. Before my trunk arrived, I only had clothes for four days.

The final numbers were in. Combining our El Salvador volunteers and the Dominican Republic group, out of 102 trainees on the first day of training, fifty-six reached their designated country. Forty-five percent of our trainees were gone after four months.

November 26, 1967, San Salvador—The Cost of Living in San Salvador

Another Peace Corps volunteer and I were bored in the afternoon, so we went to a movie. It was bad. We decided to visit a shopping center. I had developed a sweet tooth for candy because I had not tasted any since I left home. In the process, we discovered some startling facts. An eight-ounce box of chocolate cost three dollars. For me, that was expensive. I received only one hundred dollars month for all my expenses. It was a tight budget after I paid for my rent and food. I could not make this purchase every month; it was a spontaneous, luxury purchase. The chocolate items I saw were at least three times more expensive than for the same items in the USA. Anything imported was expensive here. To understand how expensive it was for me, think of someone in the USA earning $2,500 a month. Considering the cost relative to income, this would be the equivalent of paying seventy-five dollars for eight ounces of chocolate candy. For supper, we had a good steak for one dollar and sixty cents. That was one time I did not mind spending that much for a meal. After that, we decided to see another movie, *The St. Valentine's Day Massacre*, which I enjoyed. All the day's spontaneous actions cost me five dollars, or five percent of my monthly income.

When I was in Sonsonate, I would spend almost nothing, but when I was in San Salvador, my money disappeared quickly.

November 28, 1967, San Salvador—Made in Nahuizalco

Yesterday in San Salvador, I entered a large handicraft store with items ranging from machetes to chairs, lamps, and clothing. Everything was beautiful and colorful and made in Nahuizalco, the Indian village through which I walked every time I went to the *cantón* Pushtan.

December 2, 1967, San Salvador—We Rent an Apartment

Every time we volunteers traveled to San Salvador, we had to stay at a cheap hotel, which depleted our budgets. We could not afford more than one trip every two or three months. That was not enough. We needed to get away and speak English among friends. Not being able to express ourselves freely was frustrating, and we had to release the pressure. Those of us at the lower end of Spanish-speaking ability suffered more. Not being able to communicate freely was a great strain on us.

One volunteer suggested that we form a group and rent one small apartment collectively. That would decrease the cost of staying in San Salvador, and we would have a common meeting place. We found a group of seven volunteers who were interested and three more volunteers who might be interested in becoming part of our group. We could divide the rent, and each volunteer could buy a small mattress. When we were not in town, we would leave our mattresses rolled up so as not to needlessly occupy floor space. When we were in town, we would unroll our mattresses so that anyone else arriving would know who was already there. This would allow us to meet, speak English, and release frustration.

We placed one of the volunteers in charge of this project. He found a three-room apartment near the Peace Corps office and rented it. We had each left him an agreed-upon amount of money, and he conducted the business.

Even though our apartment was only large enough for ten mattresses, we could tolerate fifteen. Because we did not have enough money to visit San Salvador every month, it was unlikely that more than three or four volunteers would ever be there at one time. The only rule was that everyone had to be careful when inviting someone from outside our group into the apartment. We sometimes left cameras, clothes, or money there, and volunteers were always meeting strange people traveling through Central America. The urge to help them was strong, but we did not want to allow a stranger access to our personal belongings.

One day the Peace Corps doctor invited our group of apartment renters to his house for dinner. His apartment was located high on a hill overlooking the city. It was exquisite and had a beautiful view. We had a delicious dinner, followed by drinking aged and expensive scotch. It was a new experience for me—and not entirely pleasant. I thought that my taste buds would confirm that it was expensive whiskey, but they had no idea. My colleagues, though, could recognize its distinguished quality. They were unanimous in their rave reviews. I just took their word for it. Along with the scotch, we enjoyed pleasant music played on an expensive record player. The music was relaxing and, when considered with sipping the scotch, it was a mystical experience for me. Being amid luxury was uncomfortable for me but enjoyable.

December 22, 1967, San Salvador—Christmas Blues

As Christmas approached, I felt pangs of loneliness and a sense of loss for not being with my family. This Christmas was confusing for me because everyone was walking around in short-sleeved shirts. To see Santa decked out in the white beard and a short-sleeved blouse made it even more unreal.

That morning, I stopped by the Peace Corps office to pick up mail and to see if any of my colleagues were in town. There was no mail and none of my colleagues had arrived. The Peace Corps office was always the first-place volunteers went when they were in town.

I started walking from the Peace Corps office to our apartment. I was not in a hurry. Six blocks from our office was a hardware store. The store was playing Christmas carols over an outdoor speaker, using it to pull in customers from the street, but the music was playing so loudly that it must have disturbed the neighbors. Why the neighbors tolerated it was inexplicable to me. The speaker was of inferior quality, as was the disc used to play the music; the sound was very scratchy. Even so, I leaned against the wall of a neighbor's property and listened to three or four songs. I thought of home. It was interesting to think that these two worlds, so different, could exist simultaneously. Someone at home might be trying to start a pickup in the freezing weather, and in El Salvador, they might be harvesting pineapples, sugarcane, or coffee. It was as if I was trying to live in two places.

January 1968—No Letters Found

I started the year with going to the Literacy Education Office, my Peace Corps assignment. I still was not sure what the office's duties were, other than being responsible for improving literacy in the country. I had no idea what the plan was for increasing the nation's literacy. I did, however, learn why most of the country was illiterate—no one seemed to care. The government employees were not interested, other than for keeping their jobs. The director of the office was a disinterested and incapable drunk, but other than that, he was perfect for the job.

In two weeks of going to the office every day, I never once saw the director. He was always in meetings, or traveling, or doing something that involved not being in the office. I had become disillusioned and suspicious. I learned where he lived and was determined to surprise him at his residence, which was a couple of miles out on the other side of the city. If I wanted to talk with him, I needed to walk there.

It was hot, and my shirt was wet when I arrived at his house. I gave three firm knocks on his door. He lived in a nice house, one that could only be maintained by someone with an above-average income. After a slight delay, a maid meekly showed her face from behind a secure door that she cracked just enough for me to see one eye. I asked for the man by his name. (I cannot remember it, so I will call him Don José.)

After several uncomfortable minutes, Don José pushed the door open a few more inches and squinted out at me. When he recognized me, he seemed embarrassed. He never expected me to go to his home. My Peace Corps training had taught me to recognize the symptoms of a hangover; he was hungover. He offered no explanation, but he agreed to meet me the next morning at ten o'clock in the office. What he wanted right then was for me to go away. With his promise in my pocket, I left.

My goals were to understand my role in his agency and what I could and should be doing each day. Even if the director chose to pass each day in a drunken stupor in his house, I wanted to be productive. I wanted to visit the Las Tablas project—the one with the irrigation, vegetable production, and marketing project.

I was waiting patiently at the office the next morning at ten. By eleven o'clock, I was not waiting so patiently. By noon, I was furious. He had told me he would be at the office by ten o'clock. Much later, I was to learn that he had used a stalling tactic to get me out of his face. I stomped out of the office and stomped the entire two miles to his house. I knocked on the door even more firmly than I had the day before. The same maid peeked out again, even more timidly. As soon as she saw me, she motioned for me to wait, and she closed the door. I heard talking in the background. She reappeared to tell me that Don José had traveled to San Salvador for an emergency meeting.

He had traveled nowhere. He was drunk inside the house.

I returned to the office and spoke with Don José's secretary, asking if he knew about the Las Tablas project. He did. When I asked if he could take me there, he agreed, but only the next day—he was wearing his office clothes and did not want to get them dirty. We agreed to meet the next day at the office at nine o'clock.

I returned the next day, on time, and was surprised to find the assistant there, as promised. (I will call him Juan since I cannot remember his name either.) We drank water to hydrate our systems before walking in the sun and then we started walking toward the bus station.

Once we reached the main highway that went to Acajutla, the seaport that was eight miles away, we stopped a *pinga-pinga* bus (one that stops on demand). After three or four miles, we stopped the bus at a spot where there was a big hacienda called Santa Clara. Behind a fence and trees was a big hacienda house. On the second story there was an open patio that was bigger than the house where I rented my room. It had a large A-frame living room, with the bedrooms behind the high ceiling of the A-frame.

We walked into the working part of the hacienda. Juan spoke with the hacienda manager and asked him permission to cross his land to reach Las Tablas. There was no problem, although the manager's eyes never left me. He studied me from head to toe. I knew he had questions, but he did not ask them.

We continued our journey another couple of miles across land that had not seen rain in months. The soil was rock-hard with cracks everywhere. The vegetation was dead and brown, except for the deep- rooted trees, and there was only a half dozen of them. It was hot, and I was sweating profusely. Juan did not sweat. I now understood why we had drunk all the water we could before leaving the office.

My weight in Puerto Rico was 177 pounds; I now weighed 165 pounds. I had lost twelve pounds in forty-five days. I ate healthy food, but I was walking from ten to twenty miles a day.

A large green tree appeared on the horizon. Under it was the water spring that was supposed to improve the life for dozens of families. As I approached the tree, I saw the spring, but little water was flowing from it. The water flowed slowly, but the soil reclaimed it after only six or eight yards. I measured the flow as best I could at eight gallons per minute. On our family farm, a bad well produced five hundred gallons of water a minute. Bathtubs produced a flow of more than eight gallons per minute, yet my job was to figure out how to use this small amount of water to improve the lives of dozens of families. I was losing my enthusiasm for this project.

I wanted to speak with the community leader if there was one. Juan had difficulty locating the man who claimed to be the leader. When we found him, he did not show enthusiasm for the project. I did not understand why they had brought me to Sonsonate for this project if the office director did not want me there, if there was no water for an irrigation project, and if the community leader was not interested in the project. The national office created the project in San Salvador and forced it on the local office and the community—and neither wanted it.

February 3, 1968, Sonsonate—Looking for Community Leadership

I returned to Las Tablas four times in the previous months, and I located the local self-proclaimed leader; he wanted a fishpond for the community. I was unable to convince him that the water flow was inadequate for anything except the community's basic water needs—drinking, bathing, and washing clothes. It was unlikely to serve all those needs unless we could capture the flowing water into an enclosed concrete basin to prevent any evaporation or reabsorption into the soil. Even so, we could expect fewer than two hundred gallons a day of water. That would serve the basic needs of only a couple of dozen people.

February 4, 1968, Sonsonate—Rest and Relaxation at Atecolzol

I went to Atecolzol (ah-tae-*col*-zol), a gorgeous rural resort located only a half dozen miles from Sonsonate on the main highway to San Salvador. It had a swimming pool as large as a football field. Most of it was located under huge *ceiba* (*say*-bah) trees that were eight to ten stories tall, with branches and leaves reaching at least thirty feet in all directions from the trunks. There was an outdoor bar at its edge—in El Salvador, there were no indoor bars. In the background, visible in the open space between two gigantic trees and across the translucent fields of coffee, was the amazing and perfectly cone-shaped volcano Izalco.

It was a vista that I could not have imagined, until I saw it. Only months ago, I was on a Nebraska farm, and now I sat at a small table by the swimming pool, formed from volcanic rock with a gorgeous volcano in the background. My mind had trouble connecting the two vastly different scenarios. Forget the corn field; I could almost reach out and touch a volcano!

The swimming pool was the park's centerpiece. Springs fed the pool which had a depth from two to ten feet. Small fish were in the water, and they kissed my legs as I moved about; this was disconcerting the first time I felt them because I was not used to sharing a swimming pool with fish. Volcanic rock formed the sides of the pool. The bottom of the pool consisted of a sand-like material, a volcanic ash.

While I was at the pool, I met three American boys my age. One was a Peace Corps volunteer but had not trained with me; he was from another region in El Salvador. The other two were Mennonite missionaries. The Mennonites were working in community development somewhere in the country. Unlike the Mormon missionaries I encountered, the Mennonites were not trying to convert Salvadorians to their religion, but like the Peace Corps, they worked in community development. We said hi to each other, but I stayed with the people who had brought me. I did not think it would be correct to abandon the group of Salvadorians in favor of the three boys, whom I did not know, just because they were fellow Americans.

Weekends bored me. I often slept, even when I was not tired, just to alleviate the boredom. I needed to find something better to do. Maybe I could climb the volcano Izalco the next weekend. I could camp out on a mountain that rose above the volcano. On this mountain was a small pine forest, which was very unusual in El Salvador. It would be good to see it.

As for my work, I occupied my time by being unoccupied and looking for something to occupy my unoccupied time. I had four busy half-days each week. That gave me much unused time. This was something for which I was not prepared—the large amount of time with nothing to do, even though the Peace Corps warned me about it in training.

During the holiday fiestas, I would go to the market and spend hours bargaining on one or two items that I did not want and did not have the money to buy. For example, I now knew the prices of sewing machines, whether bought with cash or on credit.

February 5, 1968, Sonsonate—A Typical Week

I went to Pushtan to see a *campesino* about my first terrace project. Finally, I would use the bubble level that I brought with me. I was optimistic about finishing at least two or three terraces for a garden this month.

In letters from home, my family asked me how I spent my week. The following is a summary for what might be a typical week:

Monday
Monday was the worst day of the week. I usually had nothing to do, but today was special. The Education Foundation in San Salvador was to send an important emissary to view our work. We were to go to Las Tablas to make a formal site survey of the place. The intent was to place a teaching brigade there (whatever that was). That was why this important man was coming. Without him, the gathering would not be officially formal and would not count as an official meeting. Important people from San Salvador always needed to come to make an event important; otherwise, these important people would have nothing to do.

I went to the office at 8:30 a.m. There was no need to go earlier because the office director was never there. I arrived, and to my surprise, the office director was there. Unsurprisingly, the important man did not come. They now claimed that he would come next week. With nothing to do, I returned home. My workday was over.

The people in the rural area eventually would realize that we were not coming that day. There was no way to inform them, except to physically go there to tell them we were not going to be there; of course, no one would make the effort to notify them.

Tuesday
This was a huge day. We had scheduled a meeting in the afternoon in a *cantón* (township). Early in the morning, I had gone to the Agricultural Extension Office to triple-check our departure time. We were to leave for the *cantón* at 2:15 p.m.

A man from a credit association was going to talk about what documentation the *campesinos* needed to apply for special agricultural credit. The Agricultural Extension people also were going to give a synopsis of the services they offered. América would talk about what she could do for the women, and Vicente would discuss what he could do to help the men, especially if the bank accepted their credit application. I was not officially representing the Literacy Education Office, but my presence helped me to become better acquainted with the farmers and communities in the region. It also allowed me to see how other agencies operated. The more I saw, the more I understood that the literacy office was dysfunctional.

When we arrived in the community, no *campesinos* had arrived. I assumed that was because people from government agencies often called community groups to meetings, but the agencies themselves rarely appeared. No one could blame community members for not showing up for any meetings before they could confirm the government's presence in the community.

Soon, it was 3:00 p.m., the time the credit agent had scheduled the meeting to start. Not one person had arrived. América, the woman from Agricultural Extension, being determined, walked around the *cantón*, telling everyone about the meeting. She told each person to go and inform his or her friends and to be at the school for a 4:00 p.m. meeting. She made herself visible to dozens of community members so that they knew she was present. Once the community knew the government officials were present, they became curious and started to head toward the meeting place.

As we waited, a half dozen people played soccer on the school's field, while others talked in small groups. People started to arrive at 4:00 p.m., and by 4:30 p.m., we had enough people to start the meeting. Each member of the delivering group gave a synopsis of what they did. América talked about home economics. Vicente talked about crops. As the meeting continued, more people arrived. Finally, the guest speaker gave his presentation about agricultural credit. When the meeting ended, forty-three people were present.

I was impressed with América. She had taken a situation destined for failure and converted it into a success. Her enthusiasm and initiative stood in contrast to what I saw in my office director. He never appeared and never tried to do anything. Our literacy office consumed resources each month just to stay open. The largest cost was our office director's salary. These were scarce resources that the country could not afford to throw away, yet it did. The people needed all the help they could obtain. It should have been a crime to squander scarce resources, but instead, it was the norm.

After the meeting, the people lingered and talked among themselves. The topic was whether I could speak Spanish or not. I was part of the team, yet I had made no presentation. I did not look like a Salvadoran, yet I was there in El Salvador. I was very self-conscious about my Spanish, so I remained silent. I was not authorized to speak on behalf of the literacy program, and I did not understand the program anyway. Therefore, there was no need for me to speak on its behalf. I was present only to learn more about the ways the other agencies performed their duties in rural communities.

América told me that the people wanted to hear me say something. I politely declined, but they were insistent. In the end, they had me trapped. I would have to tell a joke or something to satisfy everyone's curiosity. I demonstrated my limited ability to speak Spanish by wishing them a good afternoon. They all giggled and were satisfied—they were easily satisfied. There were kind people.

Wednesday

Bob traveled to Sonsonate in the early morning for a Spanish lesson that he had arranged with someone. After his lesson, we met and caught a bus back to Nahuizalco.

After lunch, I went on to Pushtan. A man had agreed to start constructing three terraces for a garden. In addition, the community leader was to have two more farmers there so I could give my presentation on how to conserve soil. Well, my contact had gone on a religious pilgrimage and had not done any preparation work. He would not return for three or four days. I searched for the other two farmers, but alas, the leader had not contacted anyone. He thought I would not appear, although the leader and I had agreed I would always visit them on Wednesday afternoons. I think he did not believe me because government officials seldom kept their words; everyone knew that. No one was offended if people did not follow through with something they promised to do. Government workers easily gave promises, but seldom kept them.

Thursday

I went to the office to fill in forms and to talk to Vicente. We were to meet a bus at 12:30 p.m. We waited until 1:30, but it still had not arrived. (We later discovered that the bus had broken down.) The next bus would not leave until late in the afternoon, so we returned to the office.

Every time someone from another agency stopped by the office with a vehicle, we begged them to take us to the *cantón*. They always politely refused, until, at last, one agreed to take us. We went to the *cantón* and established an organizational meeting for the next week. It took ten minutes. We were back at the office by three o'clock. There was nothing to do but go home. I did not have to say a single word. For the entire afternoon, one person worked for ten minutes. That was a good day.

Friday

Since I could never find my office director at the Office of Education, I spent increased time with the Agricultural Extension people. They were much more active, and I understood the agricultural aspects of the assignment.

Although I had nothing to do during the entire morning, in the afternoon, we would go to another *cantón* to organize a group of farmers. This would take longer because it took an hour to walk each way. I did not expect the result to be any different from the previous ones. We had made an earlier visit to this cantón, and the level of community interest was minimal. People like América could do much, but people like me, unfortunately, depended on América; it was impossible for me to act alone. This was due to my inadequate language ability, cultural knowledge, authority, and knowledge of how their institutions worked. Not one person appeared for the meeting.

For every success we had, we had ten or twenty failures. Community development work was like that. We needed to find the local community leader and convince him or her of the importance of our work. Rooting out this person was far more difficult than one might imagine. It often took months. Seldom was the person currently identified as a leader the real community leader, especially if that leader was self-proclaimed.

Saturday

Las Tablas continued to be a big problem for me. People from the region around Sonsonate had bought (and were still buying) small plots of land from the hacienda Santa Clara. Their goal was to farm the land, but the soil seemed only fair. The natural spring supplied enough water for a few families to drink, but there was not enough for irrigation of even small gardens. This project was poorly conceived and even more poorly executed.

This was a newly formed community, composed of people who came from an array of various places. Some came from far away, while others came from local communities. The Las Tablas community, as it was, had no structure and little organization. Real leaders had not yet revealed themselves to us—or to themselves.

The geographic location was also not favorable. To arrive there from Sonsonate, we had to take a bus three miles and then walk two miles. The walking was in the hot and unforgiving sun. It was an undeveloped area because it had been part of a large, mostly treeless pasture. Now, the sun baked the soil, and the plants were dry. I could not imagine the area as green. The community was at the bottom of every agency's list to provide any service. No one cared about this community.

The literacy program director had adopted the community three years ago and might have achieved a small degree of organization, but he had only made promises to them—promises that he never kept. The only time he went to the area was when he had a jeep to ride in. This may have been once every two months and was never predictable. Because we never knew in advance when this would be, any attempt to organize a meeting was impossible. The jeep had to come from San Salvador and then—and only then—would the office director appear in the community to make a few pronouncements and leave. (His specialty was making pronouncements and leaving.)

In Las Tablas, some people wanted a garden, and others did not. There was no consensus on how to use the water. We needed to start focusing on what was possible.

Las Tablas had other problems. The people did not have legal possession of the small piece of land that contained the spring water and the proposed garden area. The current owner, the owner of the hacienda Santa Clara, wanted to give it to them, but it first had to go through the Education Foundation Office for legalization. The problem was that we could not receive any outside help, in terms of money or special services, unless the people had legal possession of the land. We were at a standstill.

I traveled to San Salvador to try to obtain possession of the legal title. It was Thursday, and they said they would have it by the following Monday. They said they would send the title out on that same Monday with the regional director. He would deliver the title and accompany me and the office director to Las Tablas and present the people with their long-awaited titles. It would be a historical event, one worthy of the front page in the newspaper. This alone guaranteed the presence of my office director. He always showed up if there was a chance to have his photograph in the newspaper.

The Education Foundation also wanted to install a brigade. This brigade would consist of three people: one person would be an agronomist, another would be a recreation specialist, and the third person would live there and help the people. I saw this as a half-baked plan. The need for these specialists was occasional, at best. An agronomist could aid ten communities and should not be restricted to just one. If he were really an agronomist, he would lose his mind from boredom in the first two weeks from the lack of activity and isolation.

The community did not need a recreational director. People already knew how to play soccer. They were not interested in playing anything else. Besides, the only time people played was on Sundays. Even children worked hard and did not have spare time.

As for the professional who would live in the community, there were no vacant houses. The existing houses were constructed from milo stalks, rice straw and had dirt floors, although most had four walls. Most professional people would require better housing.

The nearest place to buy food was at least two miles away and only minimal items were available there, and they would be expensive. The person would have to make regular trips to Sonsonate for food. These trips would have to be frequent since there was no refrigeration in Las Tablas because there was no electricity. Most professional people would require the presence of electricity before they would accept employment.

The regional director did not appear on Monday, nor did the deeds to the land—surprise! I visited with my counterpart, and he said that they delayed the regional director's visit until sometime next month.

I went to Santa Clara and asked the hacienda manager for permission to cross his land to reach Las Tablas. He informed me that the hacienda owner wanted to visit with me. He led me to the house and knocked on the door. When the maid answered, he told her that the owner wanted to speak with me. She led me up a flight of stairs and into the living room, where the landowner was sitting with a whisky in his hand, reading the newspaper.

When he saw me, he stood and introduced himself. He offered me a whiskey, which I declined in favor of a soda. He asked me to follow him onto the patio. He had his patio chairs and table positioned under the shade cast by a couple of huge *ceiba* trees.

He lived in a large A-frame house, a style that was extremely rare in El Salvador; a landowner living on his land, rather than in the city, was also rare in El Salvador. He proudly told me that he obtained all the wood used in the construction of the house from his ranch. That may have been why there were no trees around Las Tablas.

He wanted to know all about me. I explained that I was from a Nebraska farm. I had to explain the nature of our crop and livestock operations. He was familiar with the United States because both he and his son had obtained university degrees there. He spoke perfect English. He also mentioned that his son had served in the Vietnam War.

He explained that he was financially supporting seven hundred elementary students by paying their fees and buying notebooks. This seemed like a high number to me, but I did not question it. He said that without education, there was nothing. He explained that the project, Las Tablas, was his idea. He continued to explain that he was going to obtain more water, build a fishpond, introduce irrigation, and build a bathhouse and a place for the women to do their laundry. I should have asked how and when he was going to obtain more water. Perhaps he would bore a well.

He said all the plans were ready, but I could never find out who had these plans. I could not discover how the Office of Literacy Education and this landowner were communicating. To me, it seemed like there were three donkeys pulling a single cart, and each donkey had a different destination in mind.

After our conversation had run its course, he called his foreman and instructed him to supply me with their best horse any time I wanted. I should not have to walk to Las Tablas. As we shook hands, he invited me back to talk at any time. He was a kind-hearted man.

The manager collected me and walked away toward the corral. I hurried to keep up. He saddled a horse, handed me the reins, and motioned for a cowboy to open a couple of gates. I wondered if this would have been a suitable time to tell him that I had never ridden a horse for more than five minutes.

On the way to Las Tablas, I noticed six farmers working. I rode to where they were preparing to plant corn as soon as the rains came. They explained that they had all the water they needed, and they were going to plant the recommended corn variety. Only a few, however, would apply fertilizer, and these farmers were applying insignificant amounts—far below the recommended rate.

I talked to the *campesinos* to learn more about their operations. Out of thirty farmers who worked a combined fifty acres of land, one farmer had sufficient credit to work one acre of land. That was the reason the *campesinos* applied insignificant amounts of fertilizer; they did not have the money to buy more fertilizer. The *campesinos* had to work within the limits of their cash and credit reserves. With no credit, they had to work with their available cash. For these farmers, it implied they would apply no fertilizer or any other purchased chemicals to help produce their corn. They would control weeds by pulling by hand or cutting them with their *cumas* (coo-mas), machete-type blades modified for weed cutting.

I promised them that I would try to obtain credit for them through an agency by the following Monday. On Monday, I was sick, but that afternoon we were going to the *cantón* to discuss credit. The credit agent went out in the morning to give a talk to the community about credit. If we could obtain credit for one-third of the farmers, it would be a huge accomplishment. Next year, the number could increase even more. One limiting factor that they could not alter was that to be eligible for credit, the farmer had to own at least one acre. This restriction was a severe limitation, as many farmers rented land, and few owned one acre or more.

Back at Las Tablas, the situation was shaky. The current school director was a self-proclaimed leader. For now, I needed to work through him, but people had warned me to be careful when collaborating with him, even if he had already worked there for four years. During the last couple of years, there had been disagreements among the farmers and this school director. In addition, there used to be three teachers at the school; now there were only two teachers. He made life miserable for the third teacher until he left to become the director of another school. The teacher who left was a great person and well-liked by everyone.

I had briefly met the teacher who left, and he was excited by the community's prospects. He worked through the Education Foundation and did work teaching illiterate campesinos to read and write. He received sixteen dollars per month for this effort, in addition to his teacher's pay. He also led 4-H clubs, for which he received no compensation. The community had been improving its organization until the school director started making the dynamic teacher's life difficult, and he found a better offer elsewhere and left.

The school director refused to accept responsibility for community development. He claimed that a schoolhouse was for school and should not be used for anything else. He would not allow the 4-H clubs to meet there.

That night I spoke to this school director and self-proclaimed community leader. I asked him to call a meeting for the following Monday to form a group to guide the community's future. He first said that he could not do it because he did not work for the Education Foundation. This reason was ridiculous. He was angry because he was not collecting the sixteen dollars per month for literacy work as the previous teacher had, but he was not doing any work to increase literacy among the adults.

I was also sticking my neck out because the office director would rather wait for the government to distribute the land titles before we did anything. He told me to do the same. If I started something and could not finish it, I would be in trouble from the office director.

I had my neck out in another way. The *campesinos* told me of the need to dam a stream in Pushtan. It developed into a dam-construction project, costing $2,080, but a special US fund for community development would supply only $800; the other $1,280 the peasants themselves would supply from hand labor and materials furnished from within the community. If this failed, I people would blame me.

Chapter 4

My First Trip into Guatemala

February 7, 1968, Guatemala—Day 1

My first vacation was approaching, and I was excited. I was going to visit Guatemala. I remembered studying Guatemala in sixth grade. In my mind, I still could see the photographs of the colorful Indians in mountains from our textbook.

I had a choice of three roads to reach Guatemala City: (1) I could take the paved coastal road, which followed the lowlands into Guatemala before rising sharply into the highlands and Guatemala City.

(2) I could ride a bus for fifty of the fifty-five miles toward San Salvador before turning sharply back toward Santa Ana, El Salvador's second- largest city. From there I would go on to Guatemala—this paved road had the fastest buses, but the distance was much greater; or (3) I could take a slower bus directly from Sonsonate to Santa Ana, before turning toward Guatemala City.

The third option was the most scenic route, because it rose from sea level to more than a mile high before dropping into Santa Ana. The road was dirt but of excellent quality. The bus would make slow progress, mostly because of the steepness of the road. The road crossed the continental divide at over six thousand feet. The scenery was very picturesque. There were coffee plantations, where the coffee workers picked coffee, and the *beneficios* dried it. I chose this route. It would take four hours.

I caught an early-morning direct bus from Sonsonate to Santa Ana. I was excited but pensive. In less than an hour, I was in territory that I had never seen. My eyes darted from one side of the road to the other, trying to see everything. We were climbing slowly but steadily, higher, and higher. We were in coffee country.

I could see peasant huts on both sides of the road. As we passed each hut, I saw a snapshot of peasant life. I could see women preparing food. They might be at their grindstones, grinding corn that they had soaked overnight in water. They would grab a bit of dough and pat it into a small pancake, which, when heated on a pottery bowl, resulted in corn tortillas. As the women prepared the dough, chickens could be nearby, trying to sneak a beak full of dough.

Girls were helping the women with their chores. Boys often were kicking a homemade ball. The core of the football would be paper held into a ball shape by string ties. At this time of day, the men have already left for the fields.

As we climbed for the sky, a fog appeared and partially engulfed us, and then, as the sun became stronger, it receded again. After a couple of hours, we reached the continental divide and started our descent into Santa Ana. The road straightened, and we picked up speed.

I ate lunch in Santa Ana and started hitchhiking in the early afternoon. I had trouble obtaining a lift, but eventually, I caught a ride with a person who took me to a turn-off. The driver explained that each branch of the road continued to Guatemala City, but since he was following the road less traveled, he suggested I stay on the road more traveled. His logic seemed sound. I thanked him and left his car.

I sat on the side of the road for thirty minutes and noticed that every car followed the road less traveled. I was suspicious that my former driver might have been setting me up for a long wait, but eventually, I caught a ride on a truck. I was moving again but never for long. I managed to make it to the border (about fifteen miles) in four hours. I walked the last two miles. Even if progress was slow, I managed to spend no money in getting there. Speed was a secondary consideration to frugality. I had to make my small travel budget last.

I passed through the border with little effort. I even managed to exchange Salvadoran *colónes* into Guatemalan *quetzals*. I returned to hitchhiking. I waited for what seemed forever, and no cars or trucks passed. I was desperate when I learned that a small bus was going to Guatemala

City at 5:00 p.m. I waited and decided that spending money was preferable to spending the night on the side of the road.

The bus arrived, and the bus's loading/unloading specialists—two men—spent time loading the bus. They had empty sacks resting on their shoulders for extra protection against the heavy, sharp-edged objects they carried. Finally, we were ready. The driver started the engine, but before the driver could close the door, someone in the bus sent a child out in search of another person. Meanwhile, we had to wait. After five minutes, the child returned, tugging on the arm of a happy drunk. Two police officers helped him into the bus. Finally, we were moving again into Guatemala.

I was happy to see that the driver had a heavy foot. I wanted to arrive in Guatemala City as early as possible because I had no arranged place to stay. I thought we were making excellent time until the driver started pulling into small towns positioned just off the highway. The bus delivered people to their front doors, and frequently, they needed packages brought down from the top of the bus. As luck would have it, these packages were often located at the bottom of a pile of packages. This required the repositioning of packages to retrieve one package; time was passing, and night was approaching.

At one point on the road, there was a minor discussion between two passengers and the driver. The two passengers did not want to pay the full price. They tried to negotiate the price lower. The driver finally had had enough and abruptly stopped and opened the door. Their mouths dropped open, and one of them muttered, "Well, I still think it is too high," as they dug deeper into their pockets for the money.

Again, we were traveling and making time, and then the drunk awoke abruptly. He started making passes at a female sitting next to him. She encouraged him—not too much but sufficient to keep the drunk's mind focused on her. Suddenly, his face became serious, and he muttered something. Everyone around him laughed, and the driver suddenly stopped the bus. The drunk wobbled out and positioned himself next to the truck's back tire. He moaned in happiness as he emptied his bladder. The weight of the world was lifted from his bladder. As he turned to reenter the bus, he broke into another song.

We were gaining elevation, and it was becoming colder. I was wearing only a short-sleeved shirt with no T-shirt under it. I was already uncomfortably cold, and we were going still higher to reach Guatemala City.

We arrived at the bus depot at 8:00 p.m. I went to the police to ask directions. It was logical to ask the police because they were everywhere. They were nice and even found me a taxi. They negotiated the taxi fare as I hid around a corner. If the taxi driver had seen me, he would have charged much more.

The taxi took me to the part of town where cheap hotels were supposed to predominate. It took forever to find a nice, cheap hotel. The one I found was located near the US embassy and the central market. With that problem solved, I took on the next one: hunger. I located and ate at a nice American restaurant. That was how the first day of my vacation ended; I had arrived in Guatemala.

February 8, 1968, Guatemala—Day 2

I froze on my first night. The temperature fell to fifty degrees Fahrenheit, which, for me, was very cold. I went to the bus depot to catch a bus to Chichicastenango (chee-chee-cas-ta-*nan*-go), a village located to the north, near Mexico. This was a four-hour trip by bus. I was on a tight schedule, so I did not try to hitchhike; that was too unreliable.

I boarded a little, packed bus. They not only squeezed me in, but it seemed that half of Guatemala City entered the bus after I seated myself. When I gazed over the heads of the people already seated, I thought of a Nebraska cornfield in early July. Every time the bus moved from side to side, so did all the heads in the bus, like when a breeze moved across a cornfield—all I could see were the plants moving back and forth, according to the whims of the wind.

There was no visible aisle in the bus because people were sitting in it. I did not know how that was possible until I saw that the bus had custom-made fold-down half seats to make aisle seating more comfortable. I found an "aisle seat." I was thin, but my bottom quickly lost all sensation after fifteen minutes of one side of my bottom supporting my body's full weight. To make life more interesting, everybody had their shopping bags, chickens, and packages that they were carrying with them.

Initially, I longed for a full seat, but then I noticed that the bus had overhead compartments, like the airlines did, except these were open on the sides, and the bottoms were made from steel mesh. There was always something falling from the overhead compartment onto someone's head. Passengers placed their chickens and iguanas (giant lizards) in the overhead compartments, directly over the persons occupying a regular seat, especially the window seat. I know that these animals did not make any effort to hold it in until we arrived at our destination. People sitting below them were at the mercy of the animals' bowel and bladder movements. I did not want to finish the trip with urine or fecal material on my head and shoulders. The aisle seat no longer seemed so bad.

The trip seemed endless. The bus was slow. It was always stopping to pick up people. I did not think anyone left the bus; only more people entered it. It reminded me of putting more water into a balloon that already looked like it should have burst. I expected the balloon to burst, but it did not; it just kept expanding. The only way this bus could hold more people was for it to expand like a balloon.

As we wound around the highland roads, we still gained elevation. Before long, I started to see pine trees and scenery that reminded me of Colorado. I saw large corn and potato fields. The size of fields was relative to those found in my region of El Salvador, not to the US. It looked to me that the Guatemalan farmers were better than those I had seen in El Salvador, but the soil may have been superior.

I arrived in Chichicastenango at 1:00 p.m., ate lunch at the only place in town, and by 2:00 p.m., I was ready to match bargaining skills with the local merchants. These merchants were specialists at spotting foreign tourists and then raising their prices. My goal was to impress on them that although I was a foreigner, I was not a tourist. They were not impressed with my ploy. They could not stop seeing me as an American tourist and kept their prices high.

The merchants were surprised that I could speak Spanish—at least, a little—because most tourists could not. I negotiated as best I could with each merchant on each item. This took time. I bought nothing until I had visited all the market's stands and bargained on all the items that interested me. I then returned for the final negotiation and to make the purchases. I did well. I bargained for an item and then, when they accepted my offer, I bundled it with another item and argued again. I kept adding items until I had what I wanted for a reasonable value. I bought one item for $0.70 and then saw a non-Spanish-speaking tourist pay $2.50 for the same item. I felt proud.

In this region, the people were very colorful. They had been around American tourists enough that they could speak a little English. They knew how to say "Come in" in English, and of course, they knew the numbers.

After I had spent my budget, I caught a 4:00 p.m. bus to the Pan American Highway. This bus was very crowded, as all Guatemalan buses were. It was a sea of heads. I counted seven heads across a row of seats. In a similar bus in the USA, we seated four people. This did not include the chickens, canteens, machetes, hats, and whatever other things the passengers carried. People also read newspapers on the bus.

We reached the highway, and I was uncomfortably cold. I never imagined Guatemala would be cold. I imagined that all Central America was hot. It was the tropics.

I tried to hitchhike to Lake Atitlán (ah-teet-*lan*), which put me back on the road toward Guatemala City, but I had no luck. One person stopped who was going my way. I asked him to wait while I ran a few feet to grab my bag. As soon as I turned my back, he sped away. At least running helped me to warm up a bit.

I found a bus passing by and waved it to stop. I was surprised to see it was not crowded, but it was night, and it was near its destination. I arrived in the colorful Indian town above Lake Atitlán. I needed to continue another three or four miles to the village, located at the lake's edge. The last bus had left, and traffic was nonexistent. There were no hotels in this town. My only hope was to take a taxi. Unfortunately, the taxi driver also knew that he was my only hope. This fact did not aid my efforts to negotiate a price. It cost me three dollars to travel the four miles. I managed to find a beautiful little room for five dollars a night, which included three meals.

That night I looked over the town. I met two married Guatemalan Peace Corps volunteers. Their assignment had been in a little village near the jungle. The man worked with cooperatives. The people were nice there and wanted the volunteers' help. The only problem was that during the first ten days, the Communists had killed one of his co-op's members each day. The Communists had killed seven co-op members since he had arrived. The Communists disagreed with the cooperative philosophy. I found that surprising because I thought that communists were all about sharing and cooperating. The Peace Corps moved the couple to another site. The bus ride from their new site into Guatemala City was eleven hours.

In Lake Atitlán, flowers were everywhere. They came from bushes that grew up the sides of fences and house walls. They were all bright colors: red, purple, and yellow. Pine trees were everywhere; their fresh scent filled the air.

The next morning, I walked to the lake beach and took a few pictures. I prepared to hitchhike to Antigua (an-*tea*-gua), another Indian village known well by tourists. I waited a couple of hours in Lake Atitlán but did not find a ride from the village to the town by the main road. I eventually caught a bus that took me to the town—the same town where I had had trouble negotiating with the taxi the previous night.

I walked to the town square and piled into a little bus. I asked when we were going to leave. The response was "Right away." After I sat in cramped quarters for more than thirty minutes, we were still going to leave "right away." I returned to the robber taxis for a ride to the highway. I asked when they were leaving. They did not leave at regular intervals but when their taxi was full. If you chartered the taxi by yourself, the price was high. They were always going to leave "right away." I waited for fifteen minutes before deciding to hitchhike.

I went to the road and waited. Not one car passed me that was not full of people hanging out of the windows. After thirty minutes, I decided to try the buses again. They proclaimed they were leaving right away, but still, no one left. I tried two more buses, but the story was the same. In desperation, I returned to the robber taxi.

The taxi left me on the Pan American Highway. Since it was already afternoon, I had lunch at a restaurant. After I ate, I tried to hitchhike.

Trucks passed, but no one stopped. I waited ninety minutes before a car stopped. The driver owned a flour-milling plant and received his education in the States. He spoke perfect English. He oriented me about the political situation in Guatemala. He told me that cars were not stopping for me because they were afraid. People had been killed after picking up hitchhikers.

The driver explained there were two political factions fighting in Guatemala, the left and the right. One never knew who was responsible for what. Someone would be found dead, and no one would have any idea which faction was responsible. He said that police cars in Guatemala City always circulated in pairs, with at least two police officers per car. The police required all nonpolice cars to drive with their interior lights turned on. Police would automatically open fire on any car moving in violation to this rule. There were officers with small firearms and machine guns on street corners. Officers carried their machine guns in the ready-to-shoot, horizontal position.

My host was interesting and gave me a much better picture of Guatemala politics. In ninety minutes, we covered a distance greater than I could have covered in three to four hours of bus travel. Finally, his road and mine diverged. I thanked him profusely. He had been kind.

I was still twelve miles from Antigua, so I tried to hitchhike. Within five minutes, an American couple picked me up. They had lived in Antigua for five years. They gave me a list of places to visit. They also took me directly to a hotel they recommended. An English-speaking German woman operated it. She gave me a nice room with hot water. That was the first hot water I had felt since I was in the Virgin Islands. She also gave me a discount on prices.

It reminded me of facilities one could enjoy in Colorado or Canada, where hunters might stay. It was beautiful. Each bed had five wool blankets. I would be so comfortable, lying under those blankets at night, especially since there was no way to heat the room. The room temperature would be only degrees above the outside temperature. The best place to be in the room was in bed, under all those blankets.

I took a long, hot shower. I showered with the door closed to save the heat generated by the hot water. I dried quickly because the room was still chilly. From the bathroom, I ran and jumped into bed, pulling the covers quickly over me. I was still cold. I got up and grabbed three more blankets from the backup blanket pile and then jumped back under them. The weight from the blankets comforted me. I was toasty and happy. I immediately fell asleep.

The next day, I walked around the lake and enjoyed German cooking in restaurants. The bright sun helped to neutralize the cold. I went to see ruins, for which Antigua is noted. I hired boys as guides. I tried to hire just one boy but could not hire just one. They each had memorized their monologues in English. Once they started on it, they had to finish it. It was fun to let them complete half their presentation and then ask a question. They always had to return to the start position. The ruins did not impress me, but I enjoyed the people.

It was late afternoon, and I had not eaten. I began looking for a place to eat. While looking, I ran into another volunteer on vacation. Together, we found a small shop and ordered hamburgers. Surprisingly, they came with a green salad, which the Peace Corps discouraged because it frequently made people sick from the strange little things that lived on the leaves.

We ate and enjoyed the restaurant's food while watching the people passing on the street outside the window. That is when we saw our Peace Corps doctor pass. He saw us, stopped, entered the restaurant, and approached our table. He pointed at the salads on our plates and warned us against eating the salads. We were embarrassed but not enough to stop eating the salad. The next morning, I was fine, but my friend was in terrible distress. I had a cast-iron stomach. Those little critters could do me no harm.

I returned to the hotel, changed clothes, and took a hot shower. When I finished dressing, I returned to the park. A musical group was performing from a balcony overlooking the park. They were serenading the people in the park. The music was unusual because it centered on a xylophone, not a guitar.

The night was very chilly. The crowd was growing. I noticed that the people listening to the music had no coats or shoes. What amazed me was that they did not seem to feel the cold. They were not tensing their bodies to combat the cold. They were just standing there, as I would in eighty-degree weather. That was when part of the crowd began milling around the park while the musicians played. At first, it appeared much like cattle in a holding lot when they started to mill. Small groups of people broke rank and milled in the opposite direction. That is when I noticed that the boys were circulating in a counterclockwise direction, and the girls were circulating in a clockwise direction. I learned that this was the way that young boys and girls started courtship, by simply looking at each other in the park. I thought that we did the same thing in the States, only we used cars. Our way required gasoline, and we met fewer people. The children had adult chaperones. They were the ones who appreciated the music as the children walked around the small park's fountain. It was a clever system.

Before supper, I visited souvenir huts to discover the price range of assorted items. I located two sweet little Indian women in the square who were selling interesting things. I bargained on items, and I agreed to buy those items from them the next day at 9:30 a.m., since I was not carrying money with me. We would meet at the same place to conclude our business.

The next morning, I was sick. I had a sore throat, stiff neck, and a cough. Although my cast-iron stomach had not let me down, my walking around without adequate clothes did me in.

I met another young American doctor. He did medical research in Malaysia. He was traveling to El Salvador and offered me a ride. What a gentleman! He and I had breakfast together, and we agreed to meet at 10:30 a.m. to head toward El Salvador.

After breakfast, I went to the park to make my purchases. I had budgeted three dollars for the purchases and not one cent more. I found the girls. I expected to make my purchases quickly, as I had already negotiated the prices, but I had to start over and renegotiate every price. That disappointed me. I concluded my purchases and started toward where I was to meet the doctor. Suddenly, behind me, I heard loud, shrill screams. I turned to see two more women who looked like the women I had just negotiated with. In fact, these were the women I had negotiated with yesterday. They looked at my purchases in disbelief. They looked at me as if I had betrayed them. I was in a tight spot. I had already spent my allocated budget, but I had no choice. I spent an additional two dollars with them. That was my reserve money. Now, I needed my free ride with the doctor more than ever; without him, I would have to go to the Guatemalan Peace Corps office and beg for enough money to return to my home in El Salvador. I left immediately; I was afraid that more shouting women might appear and that I might miss my free ride home.

Later, I caught my ride back to El Salvador with the American doctor. I arrived home with ten cents in my pocket but very satisfied with my Guatemalan adventure.

Chapter 5

Back to the Grind

El Salvador, Spring 1968 (Exact Days and Months Cannot Be Identified)

Four Mormon missionaries moved into a house located only a half block away. I now lived in the American suburb of Sonsonate.

Trip to Acajutla

When I introduced myself to the director of the Literacy Education Office and tried to coordinate work with him, he insisted on doing nothing. I had not joined the Peace Corps to do nothing. I tried many ways to meet with him and learn what I was supposed to do, but none worked. Finally, one day, América invited me to join her in her work with the National Agricultural Extension Service. I presented the idea in San Salvador to my Peace Corps director. They presented it to the National Extension Service, and they approved it. I severed all ties with the literacy program and continued going daily to the local Extension Service, only now, my presence was official.

This morning in the Agricultural Extension Office was monotonous and uneventful. As usual, we had no transportation. This was enough to prevent our agronomist from leaving the office. He alleged he had a report he needed to complete.

América and I gathered our things and headed toward the *cantón* Tres Ceibas. We walked two miles from the office to the edge of town, where the main highway went to the capital, San Salvador. We waited minutes before we waved down a *pinga-pinga* bus and climbed on. The ticket taker came, and we each paid our own fares. The government did not reimburse us for these transportation costs. The more we worked, the more we traveled, and the more bus fares we paid from our own pockets. That was dedication on our part, and it was worth it to be out of the office.

The vistas were always beautiful in El Salvador. It was a green country, where layered landscapes were marked with different degrees of translucence. The vistas were clear because of the lack of pollution. This was true, except when the sugarcane owners burned the refuse on their recently harvested cane fields. Then air pollution was horrible. But for most of the year, I never tired of looking at the sugarcane fields, the coffee plantations, and the small farmers working in their tiny fields. These gorgeous vistas masked the economic and social injustices that permeated this society.

After a half hour, we came to the *cantón*. We signaled the bus to stop, and we stepped off. We crossed the road and headed inland. The school was a ten-minute walk. We saw the usual activity, with people coming and going. Dogs ran about on tasks of urgency; oxcarts squeaked down a path with the *campesinos* walking in front, issuing orders to the oxen via a stick that never broke contact with the wooden harness around the oxen's necks; and women with filled baskets on their heads went to catch buses.

We turned left at Don Miguel's tienda and saw the school. It looked empty. That was not a good sign. We had established a meeting for this time, but no one was there. América and I looked at each other, and we looked around again. The people had abandoned the *cantón*.

We looked inside the rooms and found no one. We grabbed two student desks and set them outside, where we waited and watched the movement in the community. We should have had five or six men, women, and children waiting for us.

When no one showed up, it was usually a sign that something unexpected had happened in the community. Perhaps someone had died, or they all needed to be in the fields for some reason. After forty-five minutes, we saw a young man who was part of the group. He said that no one was coming because they were busy with something. It did not matter what it was. It happened. It happened very often, in fact. We would go home and return the next week. Our day was spent. There was no way to go to another *cantón* or to find something productive to do.

América and I returned to the road and reversed the process to go home. After minutes riding, I decided I would not go to work in the afternoon. There was nothing for me to do. I told América. There was no problem. We were supposed to have spent the day in Tres Ceibas; therefore, we had nothing else planned. The truth was no one cared whether I was at the office.

I left América and the bus and walked to my house, where I had lunch. I told my landlady, Doña Maria, that I might be late for supper. I returned to the main highway and waited for a bus to the seaport, Acajutla (ah-ca-hoot-la). It was eight miles down the road. It took only five minutes before I was on the bus. It was a slow bus, but I was in no hurry. I watched people come and go, and I watched the farms and ranches we passed. There were sugarcane fields and cotton fields. From my city to the coast, the land was flat and fertile. Logically, large, and wealthy landowners owned it. In the middle of a field were small pyramids ten to fifteen feet high. The farmers drove their tractors up and over them, if possible; if not, they drove around them, crowding as closely as possible to them so as not to leave any valuable land untilled. These were remnants of pyramids constructed hundreds of years ago, but today, no one cared.

Upon arriving in Acajutla, I stepped from the bus and looked around. Acajutla was a large village, no more. It was a small and unsophisticated seaport. On the beach, just far enough up from the water that they were in no danger from the ocean, were a half dozen huts with thatched roofs, sand floors, and bamboo sides. In these huts, simple bars operated, each with a half dozen tables and a small counter for a bar, usually located in the far corner. Young ladies, who had nothing to do, hung back in another corner.

I went into the first hut, put my book about fertilizers on the counter, and ordered an *aguardiente* (firewater) and Coke. I drank slowly and read about fertilizers. When I glanced up from my book, I saw the young ladies watching me, amused and curious. When they saw that I was looking at them, they all giggled, as if on cue.

I ordered a second drink, but I closed the book and started to think. I thought about home. I missed it very much. It was so far away in distance and in time that I did not know what to do. I was less than one year into my service, not yet at the midpoint, and that fact made the loneliness I felt for home even worse.

These moments were difficult. I had to change the direction of my thoughts. I decided to go for a swim. I did not have a swimsuit, but I learned from the ladies that I could rent one. They offered to bring it out. They were helpful. The rent was reasonable, so I rented it. I went into the back where they had a room enclosed with bamboo, and even with the cracks between the bamboo poles, I changed my clothes. I took all my possessions with me to the beach for safety reasons. I carefully laid my things on the sand and entered the water.

I was a young man and not accustomed to the drink. My head was floating merrily in its own world as I headed for the water. I ran fast into the first wave, which was larger than I had envisioned. It flipped me upside down, rotated me head over tail, and deposited me near my clothes. I was happy to lie there. If that were where I was needed, I could lie there for a moment. I looked up. The sky was blue. The sun was warm. The sound of the ocean made relaxing sounds. The afternoon was still young. I was at peace with the world.

That was enough swimming for the moment. I returned to my bar. I was the only client. A bored bartender sat in one corner. In another corner, four young ladies were milling about. At this point, I noticed the young ladies did not seem to be drinking or doing anything. I ordered another *aguardiente* and Coke and sat at a table without opening my book. I looked at the ladies and smiled. They smiled back, and two even approached my table and sat down. We talked. They were nice. I did not understand what nice young girls were doing there. I asked them. They said they were working. I found that strange because the bartender only had to fix one or two drinks per hour. When I mentioned this, they looked at each other and laughed but offered no explanation. We talked about their families and my family. They asked what I was doing in El Salvador, and we talked while I drank. They helped me to feel less lonely.

Later, I decided to take another dip in the ocean. I was far less steady on my feet as I ran into the water, but I was more confident. Again, the wave was larger and much more powerful than I had expected, and it flipped me end over end and deposited me on the beach. This time, though, I swallowed water. I decided I had swum enough and changed into my clothes.

By now it was growing dark. It was between 5:45 and 6:00 p.m. At 5:40 p.m., it was afternoon. By 5:45 p.m., the birds were fluttering around like something crazy was about to happen. They chattered and flew from tree branch to line pole and back again. There were desperate to find a safe place to spend the night, and then, at 6:00 p.m., there was no light and the birds had disappeared completely.

I asked the ladies at what time the last bus returned to my Sonsonate. They said 8:30 p.m. I had more than two hours to continue my meditation before I would have to return to the ugly real world.

More people entered the bar and occupied the other tables. The two young ladies stayed at my table. I did not understand. Women had never found me so interesting before. I was pleased with myself. The men in the bar were ordering "cylinders" of *aguardiente*. These were glass bottles in the shape of a thin cylinder and contained about ten ounces of pure *aguardiente*. I contemplated doing this also. I thought and I thought, and then I ordered it. The cylinder came quickly. The women in the corner watched with interest. I opened the bottle. The women stopped breathing in anticipation; their eyes were frozen on me. I did not understand why anyone would pay so much attention to me, especially now, as I opened a small bottle. I sniffed the bottle and bravely sipped it. It was not a big sip. In fact, it was a small sip. It was, however, enough to wake every cell in my mouth, esophagus, and stomach. I had burned these cells severely, and they were not happy. I tried to keep an all-is-good facial expression for the ladies, but they knew better. It was difficult for me to conceal my gasping for air. In fact, every time I inhaled, it provided more oxygen for the fire inside me to burn brighter. When I started to cough, the ladies broke into laughter.

Not to be a wimp, I practiced my drinking of straight aguardiente. The excitement being over, the girls found other people to talk with, but they always kept one eye on me. Finally, one nudged me and said that it was 8:35 and that I might have missed the last bus out of town. I went into panic mode. I started grabbing my stuff. I found that I did not have hands enough to grab everything. I stuffed the empty cylinder into my back pocket and ran to where the bus should have been. It was not there, but I could see it up the street. I ran after it as best I could. I did not run as much as stagger. I fell forward, and my feet tried to keep pace to prevent my face from smashing into the pavement. The bus stopped to pick up people on its way out of town. I caught it—just barely. I found an empty seat in the back and sat down. Life was good.

The trip back to Sonsonate was enjoyable, except that I was now starving. It was dark, and I could see *campesino* campfires here and there in the distance. There were no lights in the countryside because there was no rural electrification. The only light in the night was either gas lanterns or campfires, which is what the *campesinos* used for cooking and light.

The bus pulled into the bus station. I staggered off and pointed myself in the direction of my house. It was almost two miles away. I tried to walk naturally, but it was not possible. I knew that people were watching me, even more than they usually did. I tried to keep them from knowing that I was drunk, but I was certain everyone knew.

As I walked, I hoped the alcohol would loosen its grip on me, but it did not. I was hungry, and it was not possible to walk in a straight line. As I drew nearer to my house, I saw all my neighbors sitting on their front steps. All my little friends were still up, and their mothers and their distrusting fathers were all there. When they saw me approaching, they stopped talking and watched me. I did not want them to know I was drunk. I focused all my energy on walking a straight line. I knew that I could not say anything, or they would know that I had been drinking. I walked straight past each of my friends who were sitting less than one yard from me. I looked straight ahead and said nothing to them. I was proud because I reached my door and turned and walked through it without falling. When I sat down to eat, I felt the tall, cylindrical bottle in my back pocket. A bottle that size and shape had only one use: *aguardiente*. The next day, I realized that everyone on the street had seen that bottle in my back pocket as I struggled to walk past them without falling. I had fooled only myself.

The Doc's Bad Behavior

I discovered that the married veterinarian—the one who shared a room with the single Spanish veterinarian—was not a gentleman. He had studied in an Italian veterinary school, where he may have picked up unpleasant habits about how he treated women. He likely had no respect for women before he arrived there.

The doc had become famous for not paying his bills. He earned around $1,000 monthly, which was ten times what I earned. He had a large bill with Doña Maria, which she could never get him to pay. She only charged him ten dollars a month for his share of the room and a similar amount for food because he only ate a few meals each week. For Doña Maria, three or four months of his unpaid bills placed a financial burden on her. He promised and promised, but he still did not pay his bill. The rumors were that he spent lavishly on his family and refused to pay the bills not related to his family.

He had no respect for women, other than his family. He drove a government jeep to perform his duties. They kept the Jeeps in El Salvador without a cab during the dry season. As he drove by pretty women in the street, he made obscene hand gestures toward them and yelled obscene phrases at them. I know this because I rode with him once. I was so embarrassed that I had to look down and away from the street. I did not want the woman we were passing to think that I was part of his tirade against women. He embarrassed me. I quickly lost all respect for the man.

Pushtan's Waterfall

In one of my visits to Pushtan, I learned of a small farmer who was very innovative. He was well known in the area for being a good farmer. I decided I needed to meet him. I asked for directions to his hut. I tried to remember the directions, but they were long and complicated and involved paths passing through fields. They included going up and down hills, through a coffee plantation, crossing at small stream near a small waterfall, continuing to a small banana plantation, and on and on. I started walking and entered uncharted territory for me. I followed a narrow path up and down hills. I passed men, women, and children, coming, and going. Men carried sacks partially filled with something; others carried *cumas*, a tool like a curved machete and used for plant cultivation; and still others carried machetes, used for everything, including self-defense. They all looked at me like I was an animal at the zoo. I was out of my environment.

I turned and headed into another coffee plantation. The coffee bushes were ten feet tall and still growing. They were under large shade trees; whose only purpose was to provide shade for the more sensitive coffee plants. It was pleasant walking through these trees and coffee bushes, while benefiting from their shade.

Suddenly, I came into a small clearing. There was a grass hut with a dirt floor. A woman was bent over a small fire in the center of the opening. Then, from my left, I saw a nude boy. His right eye caught my attention— it was protruding from the socket by an inch and was white. It looked like a few layers of skin were protruding because the eye itself was still in place. There was no way the eyelid could close, nor could he have had any vision in that eye. When I focused momentarily on his eye, I lost track of where I was going. I nearly walked into the lady's barbed-wire clothesline. I threw up my hand for protection and stopped before I did any damage to the clothesline. I begged forgiveness from the lady, excused myself, and turned to bypass the clothesline. I disappeared into the coffee plants and their shade trees as quickly as possible.

After going up and down half a dozen more hills, I came to a huge gully. I carefully followed the mud steps carved out of the dirt hillside and slid graciously to the bottom of the gully. There, I found a creek with a narrow stream flowing. I heard water falling and followed the stream up the creek. I found a small waterfall, falling twenty feet, with a pool at its base. I had heard that this was where the Indians bathed. It was private—a natural shower and bathtub. It could have been a scene in a world travel magazine. I wished that I had brought my bathing suit.

I continued my walk to find the special farmer. I do not remember finding him; I only remember the walk to find the farmer.

The Artist

There was a small American restaurant in San Salvador that all Americans frequented. I tried to stop there every few months. It was air conditioned and made me feel like I was in the US again. I always ordered a banana split; it was so good. I enjoyed waiting for my order and listening to everyone speak English. Then, my banana split would arrive. I ate slowly, savoring the moments, but I could only take so long to finish; or the ice cream would melt, even in an air- conditioned restaurant.

On one trip I noticed a gorgeous painting on the wall, done by a local painter. The scene depicted in the painting was one that I had seen many times while on my working walks around the rural landscape. I asked to speak with the restaurant owner. He knew the name of the painter—Oscar Manuel Garcia—but he did not know how to reach him; he lived across the city in a poor *barrio*. I asked him to get the painter's address if he ever visited the restaurant again.

A Peasant's Saint's Day

Each peasant had a special saint's day. It was customary for peasants to give birthday parties on their saints' birthdays to honor them. The custom was for the peasant to give the best party possible. If he hosted the best party, within his financial means, he would have good luck during the next year. Although each peasant farmer tried to give the best party, they only invited close friends.

It is important to understand what a chicken meant to a peasant family. Chickens were not just a source of meat for special occasions or for the eggs they provided most days. They represented a peasant's savings account. Chickens represented money in the bank; peasants could only dream of having bank accounts, so they had chickens. If a member of the family became ill, they could grab a couple of chickens and head to town. They could easily sell the chickens and then see the doctor. Chickens were a very liquid asset.

Shirley snagged an invitation to a saint's party. Of course, she would take Bob, but this time they also invited me. They considered us special guests. I got up early so that I could arrive early at Bob and Shirley's house. We started walking immediately. I learned that the walk would take a couple of hours. We crossed the hammock bridge and climbed the steep hill on the other side. We went down roads, up roads, and across roads. We entered coffee plantations and then exited them again. We were so far out of any territory I had seen to date that I was lost. Only Shirley knew where we were and where we were going.

Finally, we came to a fork in the road, whereupon Shirley announced that we had arrived. The dirt-floored, grass-roofed, stick-walled house was located between the forks in the road. As soon as they introduced us, we shook hands all around with all the farmers and their wives, as was the custom among peasants. Mrs. Peasant escorted us into the house and gave us each a tiny bench, about six inches from the ground, and invited us to sit down. All the other guests were outside around the cooking pot, which hung from three sticks tied together at their top over the fire pit. The women conversed in a group, while the men talked in a separate group. I did not see any drinking. This festival was too serious for drinking.

As we waited, they brought us a full glass of pineapple drink. They had removed the pineapple's outer layer and then chopped it into small pieces, poured water on it, and then poured the resulting mixture into a glass. In lieu of a blender, they cut the pineapple into small pieces—as small as they could—but the end effect was to have small pieces of pineapple floating in water; it was refreshing. We were grateful for it after our long walk, although we were all worried about the quality of the water. Still, it would be the supreme insult to refuse their drink.

Later, they brought each of us a metal soup dish with chicken soup and a metal spoon. The spoons had rusted, thus giving the soup a rusty taste. It was imperative that we consumed the soup with a smile. We all knew this. None of us would betray the soup's rusty taste. They gave us these special utensils because of our status as special guests. The other guests had bowls made from pottery and spoons made from wood.

We each had a piece of chicken in our soup. By piece of chicken, I mean half a leg or half a thigh. It was not a full piece by our standards in America. There were too many people and too few chickens. I am not sure if they used one or two chickens for the party, but they used all they felt they could safely spare. A responsible parent never would spend so much on a party that it would put the family at risk. A peasant's chickens were also like a health insurance policy. In the peasant's world, children could quickly become sick, and when they did, they needed their chickens to pay for medical services.

When we finished, we returned our soup dishes, and we complimented the peasant's wife on her cooking. She blushed, smiled, and lowered her head in humility. We saw our host remove anything left in our bowls onto small plates and give it to their children to eat. They chewed on our bones. After the children cleaned the bones, what remained went to the dogs. The dogs were very skinny. At this time, they served us coffee. It was horrible coffee, but we all drank it with smiles on our faces. I doubt they drank coffee normally and did not have experience preparing it. We knew that we were being honored, and we could never permit any of our actions to appear to disrespect our hosts.

Our hosts had thrown a magnificent party. I cannot imagine how they could have done more to honor us or their saint. We felt truly honored.

Starting a New Year in Communities

The Agricultural Extension system started each year by evaluating the progress in the communities worked the previous year and the potential for progress during the next year. Due to our not having any transportation, other than buses and our feet, we could only work in one community per day or five per week. Our system required us to visit each community on a specific time and day each week, until the next evaluation at the beginning of the following year.

If we had an open day, Vicente and América would pick candidate communities. Only they could do this, as I had no knowledge of the local region. Somehow, they would select a community, and we would visit that community every week at the same time on the same day to generate consistency and build trust within the community. We walked around the community, talking with farmers, their wives, and their children. Our goal was to have a group of farmers, a group of women, and a group of young people in every community. The adults formed informal groups, but we organized the young people into 4-H clubs.

América and Vicente agreed that the community of Los Almendros (ahl-men-dros) held potential. We set aside one day of the week and spent it visiting this community. We were constantly looking for the person who might be the leader. We walked around and spoke with men and women. The community had a new school with grades one through six.

We stopped and spoke with the teachers. One held promise as being a leader. He spoke well, was interested in the community, and had ideas that he wanted to implement in the school.

América and Vicente decided to call a meeting the next week at the school to address the community's needs. They informed the teachers, who spread the word through the children, about next week's meeting. We visited the local *tienda* owner, Don Miguel, and informed him of the meeting so he could also spread the word.

The following week, we arrived a couple of hours early and spread out to make our presence known. We reminded people about the meeting. When it was time for the meeting, only a dozen or so people were present. Vicente gave the talk for the men's group; América gave the talk for the women's group, and I gave the talk for the 4-H group. My Spanish was improving. My talk was not perfect, but everyone understood it. We asked them to spread the word and said that we would meet again the following week at the same time.

The next week we arrived early and spread the word of our presence. At the meeting, two or three dozen people were present. We again made our presentations, and we set a meeting for the same time the next week.

On the third week, we repeated our procedures and went to wait at the school to evaluate our results. If the community did not show major signs of interest, we would abandon the community and try another. The time for the meeting arrived as did one hundred people. We made our presentations, and the people seemed interested. América said that we would start our work in the community the following week. She asked, however, that everyone meet us at the school so we could sign up the men, women, and children, each for their respective groups. At this disclosure, an uneasy silence enveloped the room. After a long pause, one man asked what we would do with these lists. Vicente said that we would send the lists to San Salvador to the Ministry of Agriculture for their records. There were no more questions, so we adjourned the meeting and agreed to meet again the next week. We returned home excited and triumphant. That community showed more interest than we expected.

The following week, we each had our lessons prepared for the community. Vicente and América had the necessary paperwork with them to sign up everyone, as required by the Ministry of Agriculture. We left the bus and started our walk to the schoolhouse. Immediately, something seemed off. We saw no people, no horses, no oxen, no children; I do not think we even saw any birds or dogs. We continued to the school, commenting among ourselves how strange it was. At the school, no one was present. We pulled chairs out on the school's patio and sat down so people could see us. There were no people. We waited an hour and saw no one. Confused, we retraced our steps to Sonsonate. We had no explanation for what we had just witnessed.

The Communist Revolution of 1932

I had to wait three years before I understood what had happened in Los Almendros. In early 1969, an American appeared at my residence. He was a PhD candidate in history from Harvard University, doing his dissertation on the Communist Revolution of 1932. This revolution occurred in the Pushtan, Izalco, Nahuizalco, and Sonsonate areas of El Salvador. The 1930s was a time of world economic depression. Every country in the world suffered. The Indians were hungry and sick, and the world's economy was crashing around them. They saw no hope for improvement. This left them open to the idea of bringing about radical change.

Even though they had only their agricultural tools for weapons, they were ready to raise them in protest. The government became aware of this unrest, labeled the Indians as Communists, and set out to crush the Communists. They sent well-armed National Guardsmen and army soldiers to do so. In the process, the National Guardsmen killed between ten thousand and thirty thousand Indians. Many of these fell in the streets of Nahuizalco, where witnesses said that the streets ran red with blood— so much so that in 1967, there were few older adult males in the local Indian population.

The Harvard graduate student had gone to Pushtan and tried to interview Indians who had survived the massacre, as it became known, but no one would talk to him. He found a wall of silence. He learned that I had been working in the community. He sought me out so I could provide him with an introduction into the community. He hoped that with this introduction, the Indians would trust him and tell him their stories of the event.

How did this event in January 1932 relate to our event in 1968? In the early 1930s, several Turkish men appeared in the region and began to organize the Indians. These Turkish men were registered Communists. They were open about this fact, but the Indians had no idea what a Communist was. They wanted change, and the Turks were offering change. The Turks were white, tall, and spoke bad Spanish. They walked around the villages and rural communities, always trying to organize, and spread their political views. As soon as they had a respectable following, they took their names and sent them to their San Salvador Communist offices.

The problem was that the El Salvadorian generals intercepted these lists. They gave the lists to their guardsmen and soldiers, who were happy to hunt the Indian peasants and kill them and, sometimes, their families.

Here is the connection: Vicente had a white complexion. I was white, tall, and spoke less-than-perfect Spanish. We walked around the area, trying to organize the people, and finally, we asked to take a list of names and send them to San Salvador. For the local citizens, there were too many similarities not to run for their lives. I thought it was interesting how one fact that had occurred thirty-six years prior—two generations—and the citizens still remembered and feared it. We eventually overcame this misunderstanding, but it took persistence on our part.

Merging Offices

The Agricultural Extension people—Vicente, America, our night security guard, Vilma, and I—had a rented office space. At another location, the two vets, a livestock specialist, and their secretary rented another office space. Someone in San Salvador had the crazy idea that we should move together and capture all economies from renting one space instead of two.

That is why we all moved to a new and less convenient location. For me, it was farther from my home, but it was for the greater good. That was when I saw the most beautiful woman I had ever seen in El Salvador. She looked like I imagined an Indian princess would look. She was no more than twenty years old, with a perfect body. She dressed impeccably every day. She must have had her long black hair and nails done every week. She always smiled but was quiet. She was the livestock people's secretary.

I learned from América that she was the mistress of the office director, who was married and had three children. His arrangement with the secretary was common knowledge. There was no attempt to hide it. It was only a couple of months after our offices merged that it became obvious that she was pregnant. There were no uncomfortable moments. She received the same respect that we extended to the office director's wife.

I liked being around the Spanish vet. He was a gentleman, and I always enjoyed talking with him.

Chapter 6

The Surprise

My Family Arrives

One day I was walking home after work. It was minutes away from dusk when a large, modern taxi appeared on the street. This was unusual because there were no taxis that new or that large in Sonsonate. It was obvious that that taxi was from San Salvador. The scene was so unusual that I stopped walking in the street and backed up to the curb to stare at the passing car. When the car passed me, I could have sworn I saw Mom, Dad, and a couple of more people in the taxi. I yelled at them, but they were already too far to hear me above the street noise, and they were out of sight in only seconds.

There was only one place that taxi could be going at that time of day: The Hotel Sonsonate. It was not a large hotel, but it was the best hotel in Sonsonate. Although I was no more than ten minutes from my house, I turned and ran toward the hotel, which was at least a mile away. When I approached the hotel, I saw the taxi there. The driver was unloading bags. I entered the hotel and saw Dad. It was smiles, hugs, and kisses all around. They had brought my two younger sisters, Shelli, and Sheri. When I returned to my house, much later, and told Doña Maria what had happened, she was happy for me. She fed me, and I slept. The next morning, I went to the office and told everyone. They all were happy for me and congratulated me. They all wanted to know when they could meet my family.

América and I had an appointment to go to a community that day. We decided to go, but we would stop to visit my family to see if they had rested from their trip. They were up and eating breakfast at the hotel. América suggested they change into comfortable clothes and accompany us to the community.

We stepped outside the hotel. We were conspicuous tourists. I felt uncomfortable with all eyes on us. América flagged a bus to the main highway. To say that people stopped to stare while we boarded the bus was the understatement of the day. Traffic in all directions backed up until we seated ourselves, and the bus started. Mom and Dad and the young ones did not seem ecstatic about their unfolding adventure. I did not know how Mom and Dad had envisioned our time together would be but riding in a common bus to visit a peasant village was not likely it.

Once we arrived at the main highway, we left the city bus and waited for our bus going to Los Almendros. My family seemed uncomfortable by standing in the street, vulnerable. I was busy translating back and forth. We caught our bus to Los Almendros. I got everyone seated in the bus. América and I sat behind them so we could keep an eye on them. It was interesting to watch them look out the windows at the greenery. We had the coffee plantations and the volcano Izalco in the background on one side and the sugarcane plantations on the other. They were silent. I would like to think that the scenery overwhelmed them, but they were scared out of their minds and saw little.

We arrived at Los Almendros, left the bus, and started walking inland to the school, our base of operations. People we met stopped and stared. Some even asked us who the people were. When they learned, they followed up with the same questions that people would ask a thousand times before my family returned to the States: How did they like El Salvador? How long were they staying? After a while I did not translate the questions, I just answered them. It saved me the headache of translating.

At the school, it was recess time. The teachers had placed a ping-pong table under a gigantic *ceiba* tree, and a school tournament was in progress. Children gathered around the table three or four children deep, laughing, cheering, and jumping up and down. In the background was Izalco, the majestic volcano. The school director yelled to get the students' attention. All students stopped cheering and playing and turned toward the school director. They also saw América and me with the four strangers. Their mouths opened, and they waited for the explanation that they knew was coming.

The school director explained that these were my mother, father, and two sisters. The children ran toward us and encircled us the same way they had encircled the ping-pong table. The questions began.

The difference in Mom and Dad's life just two days prior and what they confronted during these moments could not have been greater. Mom and Dad controlled their world in the States, but in El Salvador, they could not speak or understand the language. They were descending into culture shock.

Mom and Dad were impressed with the teachers, especially the school's director, Napoleón. They noticed the respect that the teachers had from their students. The schoolyard consisted of nothing more than a small area with the ping-pong table. There were no swings or exercise equipment. The physical area available outside the school building was small. It was too small for anything other than tiny soccer games with only two or three people on each team. That was why the ping-pong tournament was so popular.

We returned to Sonsonate. I had dinner with the family at the Sonsonate Hotel. Everyone was happy to be in a place where no one stared at them, and they could relax. We planned our time together. We would spend one more day in Sonsonate and then return together to San Salvador. After a couple of days in San Salvador, we would all fly to spend a week in Mexico. I was able to get approval for this travel from the Peace Corps office.

Doña Maria wanted to prepare a meal in my family's honor, but she lamented that she did not have time away from her tienda, and her table and stove were too small. América also gave the same reason, and they were both sincere in their offerings. Later, at the office, the Salvadorian vet offered to prepare a dinner in honor of my family. I did not want to accept because I did not like the man, but I did not want to offend him. I felt trapped, but I accepted anyway. I dreaded that night as it approached. I knew that he and his entire family were insincere and untrustworthy; in this land, honor was everything.

By the time we left for San Salvador, I was suffering from migraine headaches. The constant translating and extra care needed to meet the needs of four people, who were constantly in uncomfortable situations, was beginning to take its toll. Always the Peace Corps volunteer—trying to save money—I bought everyone tickets on the 6:00 a.m. direct bus from Sonsonate to San Salvador. It was an old Greyhound bus. The seats still reclined, even if they had breaks in the cushions. The air conditioning worked if the people would just not open their windows. I always felt like I was traveling first class when I was lucky enough to take this bus. I hoped that my family did not feel uncomfortable.

In San Salvador, we had a couple of dinners with people who insisted on giving them. I do not remember who they were, but the dinners were always beautifully laid out on a nice dining table, with the meal served by maids as everyone sat at the table. They offered us wine, whiskey, sodas, or fresh fruit juices. My family recognized the quality of these dinners and the friendship behind them. I was happy and felt honored that someone would go to so much work and expense for me and my family.

The night for the dinner with the vet and his family arrived. I had been nervous all day and already had a strong migraine. We took a big taxi to the vet's house (five of us, plus the driver). My head felt every bump in the road. As we were getting out of the taxi, two young ladies left the vet's house and walked down the street, away from us. They must have been the vet's daughters. I thought their parents had sent them to the local tienda to buy something needed for the dinner, but they never returned. That was an indication of the lack of respect they had for us. His daughters were too good to meet my sisters.

I approached the door and knocked. A maid answered and ushered us in. The food was already on the small, portable table placed in the living room. The vet and his wife immediately had us seated. The meal was spaghetti and sauce; just spaghetti and sauce—and cold at that. As soon as the maid showed us to the table, she left for the evening. The vet asked us to start eating. His wife was facing us as she leaned against the back of a sofa with a forced smile on her face. The vet was next to her with the same smile. The spaghetti was mushy. My headache was approaching the exploding point. I had to keep smiling, eating, and translating. I asked my family not to delay in eating so that we could try to escape as quickly as possible.

I still had not mastered the subtle art of cultural interpretation, and I realized that I had misread the vet's invitation. He had not wanted me to accept his invitation. He only extended it to be magnanimous. I was supposed to have declined it. The vet had shown extreme disrespect for me and my family. I would never forget it.

We finished our meal as quickly as possible, said our goodbyes, and looked for a cab. I had never been in such extreme pain from a migraine. I could stand only with difficulty. The Peace Corps doctor had told us to carry his telephone number in our billfolds. We stopped at a payphone, and I called him. He agreed to meet us at the Peace Corps office. He examined me and gave me a shot to relax me and allow me to sleep.

The Peace Corps doctor suggested that we stay at an American place, Casa Clark. It was not a hotel or motel but a *pensión*—a huge one-story house with rooms around the outside edge. It had a wonderful kitchen, with excellent American food, combined with Salvadorian food and fruits. The living room was gigantic. It had the most wonderful wooden floors; they were dark with wide boards. There were easy chairs, sofas, and small wooden tables with chairs spaced throughout. There were table and floor lamps everywhere. The overall room was dark, but each spot had more than enough light to read a book, play cards, or have a nice chat with a bottle of wine or glass of whiskey. When I looked across the room, I expected to see Ernest Hemingway drinking a glass of whiskey, while reading a book with his spectacles placed low on his nose.

It was the perfect place to rest. The Peace Corps allowed me three days to recover. I saw my family relax also. The last few days had placed strain on them as well. During the days, we saw much of San Salvador, with the aid of a VW bus that we rented. We always tried to be back at Casa Clark for meals. I had never eaten so well. The other customers were always chatty, and Mom and Dad could always find a conversation with someone interesting.

My Family Visits Mexico

We flew to Mexico City and spent the first night there. I was not prepared for a city that was so large and sprawling, with wall-to-wall people and with so much movement. The streets had no traffic lanes.

Wherever a hole appeared in the traffic, a vehicle appeared and filled it. That vehicle could have been a bus, a truck, a car, a horse cart, an oxcart, or a person pushing a food cart or transporting goods on a small wagon or wheelbarrow. The noise level was unprecedented, with so much horn honking and people yelling. It scared me. I already missed Sonsonate.

Dad hired a large taxi for the day. We went to the Indian pyramids outside of Mexico City. What amazed me about them was that they were spread out. We walked. The sports field surprised me with its vertical hoop. If I remembered correctly, they sacrificed the losers at the end of the game, or maybe it was just the losing team's captain. Wow! That would have discouraged me from entering the sports profession.

We ate in nice restaurants and stayed in delightful hotels. Dad enjoyed himself. The family enjoyed this part of the trip much more than the practical details of encounters with the poor people. I was not dragging them around to visit odd places and meet poor people who asked the same questions. I, however, had a different reaction. I felt like a traitor to my cause. I had walked great distances to save on a bus fare or negotiated vigorously on the price of a souvenir to save a dime, and here the family was, easily spending more than a hundred dollars daily. My family had worked hard to earn their money, and I did not begrudge their spending money. For Dad, it was a trip of a lifetime, and he had earned every smile, hundreds of times over. It was my problem for having the feelings that I had. I did not understand them. They confused me.

We drove to the city where the Russian revolutionist Leon Trotsky had met his end. I found that interesting—to be at the actual site where they made world history. We drove to other major tourist places. I do not remember the details, except for our trip to Acapulco.

I did not enjoy Acapulco. It was too elitist for my Peace Corps culture, but my family enjoyed it. They did not need me to translate because all guides spoke excellent English. We visited all the sites, including the man doing the high dive from the rocks. It was impressive in an unimpressive way; I saw no purpose to it. The hotel was fantastic. I always took hot showers. Those I could appreciate, even if it were elitist. The food was also excellent, but I did not enjoy the crowded restaurants, five people eating from a table that normally would have accommodated two people. That was Mexico at the peak of tourist season.

We drove back to Mexico City. I loved viewing the countryside, watching the terrain and economy slowly change. We spent one more night in Mexico City before I flew back to El Salvador. It was difficult to say goodbye again, but I did it. In the end, I do not think my sisters were impressed with anything. They had not wanted to leave their friends at home. I could not criticize them. Dad thoroughly enjoyed himself because he was an adventurer at heart. Mom was somewhere between the girls and Dad.

Chapter 7

Back in El Salvador

June 15, 1968—My Return to Sonsonate

I went to the airport, where I caught my flight without incident. The flight was long enough that I could start to miss my family. I had just become accustomed to living the life of a lone wolf when I understood that I was not a lone wolf but a member of a pack. I missed my pack.

I hitchhiked from San Salvador to Sonsonate. I dragged with me two heavy suitcases, a full paper sack, and one precious box of cookies. I arrived in my stuffy little room by six in the evening. It felt good to be in my own territory again; as humble as it might be, it was all mine.

It had rained heavily during the last week, which destroyed our demonstration plot that we had planted at the school to instruct the students about best practices. Forever the optimists, they had already replanted it. The initiative they showed encouraged me. I suspect that the teacher, Don Napoleón, at the Los Almendros school was responsible for this. Every time I went to the school, the students and teachers asked me about my parents. Don Napoleón always asked about *Don* Harold and *Doña* Viola. *Don* is a title of respect for men, and *Doña* is a title of respect for women.

June 20, 1968—The Malnourished Child

Don Napoleón was walking to his home in Izalco when a thief assaulted him on the sidewalk. When he resisted, the thief shot him. He went to the hospital where the doctors expect him to recover, but his wounds will take time to heal. El Salvador had the highest homicide rate in the world.

I was positive that a very dark cloud was following me. I was feeling mentally sick. My work was at a standstill due to Teachers' Day and a *fiesta* in Nahuizalco. They celebrate Teachers' Day by letting school out on Friday and all the following week. After they return, they have a week of exams, and then the term ends. Most of my work was in Nahuizalco, so when they were on vacation, my work ceased.

The Teachers' Day celebration provided the *campesinos* with a reason to drink until they collapsed in the streets, sidewalks, doorways, bushes, or on park benches. Drivers needed to be vigilant to avoid running them over. Sometimes, I saw two or three drunks sharing a spot on the ground, even next to sleeping pigs or chickens scratching for food. It was common to see a man's wife and children sitting in the shade near the father, waiting for him to awake and become sober enough to walk home together.

I was in San Salvador and was hitchhiking back to Sonsonate when a married Peace Corps volunteer couple gave me a ride. They were taking barrels to their village for a public health demonstration. They offered to take me to see their village. It was close to the highway and would not delay me more than one or two hours. I found their offer agreeable.

We were eating lunch in a small sidewalk café when a nurse approached us. She asked if we were returning to San Salvador any time soon. The couple replied that they would be leaving within twenty minutes. The nurse asked if they could take a child to a hospital there because she had two broken ribs. The nurse motioned for an Indian lady, who was expecting a child, to approach with her thirteen-month- old baby. The side of her head was black-and-blue. We could not see the baby's ribs because her parents had wrapped her in a blanket. Her feet, however, were exposed, and we could see they were black-and-blue, with pieces of flesh hanging down.

The female volunteer said that she had seen cases like this. Malnutrition and parent brutality typically caused them. I did not see much of this in my work, but Shirley confirmed that she had seen this often in her work in the countryside. This was typical of El Salvador's peasant poverty. The worst months for this were from December to May—the dry months. When the rains came, fruits and vegetables became more abundant, peasants' diets improved, and cases of malnutrition abated.

Yesterday was a boring day from the beginning. I went to work to discover that the head of the office—the director for the livestock part— had decided we needed to move to another office. This was a surprise to me. When I arrived, one desk was already missing—mine— so I found an empty desk and sat down. Within five minutes, they came and carried away that desk. I had no place in the office to sit. I saw one of the veterinarians' jeeps and settled into the back seat to read. Within minutes, the vet, who was responsible for that jeep, had to leave on a job. I did not have any place to sit. It was then that my amigo Bob, the volunteer from Nahuizalco, came by and suggested we go to Acajutla to play Frisbee on the beach. Finally, there was something for me to do. We left.

The next morning, everyone—and I mean everyone—asked me where I had been the day before. Usually, they did not notice if I was gone.

July 4, 1968—The Little Girl

Last Wednesday evening, I came home, showered, and retired to the outer tienda to wait for supper. I always leaned a chair against the wall and pulled out a Spanish book, opened it to a random place, and studied. As customers entered the store, I might look up to see who it was, but mostly, I studied my book. Then, I noticed a little girl enter the store. She looked like she could be eight years old, maybe ten. She asked for *frijoles*, but there were none. My landlady informed her that she was expecting a shipment any minute, but it had not yet arrived. I noticed that the little girl was neat and clean. It looked like her long, straight black hair had just been washed, and she had a contagious smile, one that caused anyone who saw it to instinctively smile too.

She said something to my landlady and pushed herself from the counter that she had been leaning against. She exited the same door she had used to enter the *tienda*. As she reached the sidewalk, she ran into the street by crossing upstream. She should have seen it, but she did not. There was a huge thump, followed by the release of air brakes. Microseconds later, I saw a blur pass outside the second door in the *tienda*, followed by screams from the women in the street.

I did not need to see what had happened. I already knew. I could not tear myself from my chair. Within seconds I heard a woman running toward us from where the girl was headed. She was desperately yelling, "Lupita, Lupita!" I could not bring myself to watch more. I retired to my room to try to think of something else. I played records to drown the cries.

July 5, 1968—A Peace Corps Colleague Dies

About ten days ago I went to Nahuizalco to visit the *campesinos* in Pushtan. After we concluded our business, Bob and I went to Acajutla to swim and take part in local refreshments. I was now twenty- one years old. It was good to laugh and speak English. Bob would be leaving soon, and I would leave in fifteen months. He asked me what I would do when I returned to the States. I had not thought about it. Until now, the act of leaving had never crossed my mind. I had just arrived, but now I started to give it consideration.

The next morning, I went to the office. As I approached my desk, I saw a telegram. I picked it up and panicked when I saw the word URGENT on the envelope. I opened it, and its message was "Come quick! Alex is very grave!" I showed it to América and ran to pack a few things and hitchhike to San Salvador. I had a tough time hitchhiking. It took forever to catch a ride, but I caught one with a couple of married missionaries. They had already served four years and were excited about returning home in thirty days. We talked mostly about their excitement of returning after living so long in El Salvador.

As I traveled to San Salvador, I thought that Alex could not be sick. Sickness does not work fast. He must have been in an accident. Alex was an intelligent young man who had graduated from a top university on the East Coast. He was a lawyer. His assignment was in the poorest *barrio* in San Salvador. I had heard rumors that his living conditions were the worst of any volunteer in El Salvador.

Walking toward the Peace Corps office, I walked faster and faster. I found volunteers already there. I asked what had happened to Alex.

They told me that Alex had died. He had committed suicide the previous morning and had never regained consciousness.

July 7, 1968—Dealing with Death

All volunteers and staff were upset. They notified the family. The embassy managed to keep the news out of the newspapers until all volunteers arrived from their rural sites. We lived with him for fifty-one weeks; we shared the most important experiences of our lives together, and hence, we had many of the same experiences. We thought we knew each other as only people can after going through basic training together. No one ever suspected that Alex could do such a thing. Mostly, we were sad that he had suffered alone.

The Peace Corps had a simple service for him that night at a Protestant church in San Salvador. After the service, we went to the funeral home for a short viewing and for us to say our goodbyes to him. Since there was a bus strike in San Salvador, Peace Corps jeeps brought his Salvadorian colleagues from his site to the funeral and the viewing. The Peace Corps insisted that we stay another day in San Salvador.

They hired a psychiatrist to lead a discussion about what had happened. Their concern was that there might be one or two other volunteers among us who might have considered suicide. They were worried that with one volunteer following through with the idea, it might make it more acceptable to others and create a chain of events that no one wanted. The discussion was productive, soothing, and necessary. It helped everyone. There was much red tape with repatriating the body to the USA because the embassy was already using all its resources in preparing for President Johnson's forthcoming visit to El Salvador. The Secret Service and CIA arrived by the plane loads. There were many men to house. They took over the two best hotels in San Salvador. They even moved guests with long-standing reservations to alternative—and inferior locations.

These men had short haircuts, wore sunglasses, dressed the same, and talked constantly into walkie-talkies. They were not difficult to spot around the city.

One of our apartment mates found a castaway American walking the streets with no place to stay. He alleged that his Harley-Davidson motorcycle had broken and was in a shop being repaired. I say alleged because when we later spoke about our interactions with him, his story was slightly different to each of us, and sometimes, it was completely inconsistent. He was a little too "hippie," and he could not sell the image. He dressed like a hippie and talked like he thought they talked, but when we looked at him, we did not see a hippie. We saw a CIA agent trying to infiltrate a group of Peace Corps volunteers.

I should provide a backstory. The embassy's security detail for the president called our Peace Corps director and told her to send over a list of the volunteers who would protest the president's trip. She flatly refused. I liked her. Although most of us were not fond of LBJ, El Salvador was not the place to protest. We all loved the Peace Corps and would never embarrass it or do anything to jeopardize our work there. It was the next day that the hippie appeared and magically crossed paths with one of us. The Peace Corps had already asked us to welcome stranded people into our apartments as part of the relocation program after the embassy occupied the hotels.

The protesting students shut down the university.

We went to the airport to see Air Force One land. It was a 737. I must admit that I felt immense pride when it landed, even though I disagreed with the policies pursued by LBJ. There was much pushing to gain a better position to see LBJ. Short people had no chance.

I learned that all US government employees would have a chance to see Johnson at the embassy when he gave a speech. We were excited, but I had not brought my suit from Sonsonate. I had to rush back to Sonsonate to retrieve my suit and hurry back to San Salvador. That was my third round-trip in one week between Sonsonate and San Salvador.

All the male volunteers from the apartment traveled together to the embassy. We found an advantageous position. What I noticed was the feeling of power in the room. I cannot describe it, but its presence was as real as that of the Secret Service. I do not remember what the president spoke about, but it was a good speech. We also saw his wife, Lady Bird, and their younger daughter, Lucy.

When we returned to the apartment, we noticed that the hippie had gone. It was a Sunday. I doubt that he could have picked up his motorcycle at a repair shop on a Sunday evening. He most definitely was a CIA plant in our apartment.

July 8, 1968—Difficulties with Vicente

I went to the office and received a very frosty reception from our agronomist. Last week there was a two-day national meeting in Santa Tecla, and I missed it. He seemed not to take into consideration that a friend had committed suicide and that our president had come for a visit. All I could do was to continue doing what I already had been doing: work with America. If she was happy, I was happy. Vicente did not seem to like collaborating with females, and I had chosen to work with America, so I imagine he preferred working alone rather than with us. There was nothing we could do, since he was the director for the Agricultural Extension Office.

July 12, 1968—Napoleón Improves

Don Napoleón continued to improve. He was shot with a .22-caliber pistol from two to three feet. Since he lunged at his shooter, the bullet entered the top of his shoulder and exited his side near his elbow.

July 14, 1968—Girls' Softball

Since this week was the National 4-H club week and today was Day of the Land, I had prepared a talk on soil conservation. I gathered my things and left. I had a slow bus and arrived at 10:30 a.m. for a 10:00 a.m. lecture. No one noticed because the girls were in the middle of a softball tournament. I watched them for a while and saw that they were good. They obviously had practiced, and by the number of excellent plays they made, I know they were familiar with the rules and had a superb teacher.

July 17, 1968—Mormon Missionaries Move in Next Door

Four Mormon missionaries moved into a house that was located only a half block away. I now lived in the American suburb of Sonsonate.

Two days ago, I spoke with our teacher friend Don Napoleón. He said that he needed another surgery because the wound was not closing.

I was listening to music and viewing my photo albums. By doing this, I made a trip home—at least in my head. It might sound strange, but lately I had not missed home. When I was busy at work, I did not have time to miss it. It should not be a surprise since I had been away from home for one year and speaking mostly Spanish for nine months.

July 18, 1968—Don Napoleón Helps Students Financially

Don Napoleón and I reached a point in our relationship where we spoke very frankly with each other. This was rare. The only other people with whom I reached this level of friendship were América and Doña Maria.

Don Napoleón told me that a group of teachers attempted to keep a few sixth- grade students in school by supplying them with notebooks and any other purchased supplies they needed. He was discouraged because they inevitably still left school. He said that they did not want to be given anything and developed an inferiority complex before leaving school anyway.

The students who finished sixth grade should have been better able to conduct business transactions or even maintain a bank account. Even small farmers buy seed and fertilizer and sell crops. They need to know how to count money. Unfortunately, they had no hope of obtaining a better job. Even the one student in one or two hundred who can continue to the ninth grade could not hope to obtain a better job because employers would give preference to city students. There were not enough jobs to satisfy all the city students. I knew of no jobs, except for manual labor, that male Indian students could expect, even with a ninth-grade education. Female Indian students would still only be able to work as maids and make eight to twelve dollars per month. Rural students in this region were typecast—they were Indians; they were peasants. That was all any potential employer could see.

Today, a student came to me and lowered his head. He informed me that he would be leaving the 4-H club because his father had found a job on a ranch at the base of the Izalco volcano. He had to accompany his family. He was sad because in this community he was an officer in our 4-H club, and there, they did not even have a 4-H club. Sometimes, I questioned if our work ever achieved anything, but this young man's attitude confirmed that we did. We gave our club members some degree of hope and helped to build pride in them. I was sad that he had to move but happy we had had an impact on his life.

During National 4-H Club Week—this week—we decided to visit the homes of our 4-H club members. All the houses where they lived were small and had dirt floors. The walls varied from milo stalks to mud bricks, to mud bricks covered with a smooth coating of mud- plaster. Some houses were neat, and some were not. A large house would have the floor space of two small bedrooms. In it, there might be two homemade beds. Eight to twelve people would usually live in the house. The roofing material varied from grass to sheets of metal, and a few even had mud tiles.

Since we always saw the students at the school, it was easy to not think about where they lived. Plus, for the first time, I realized that the students had no books. They only had notebooks to take notes in from the lectures that the teachers gave. When I mentioned this to Don Napoleón, he told me that the teachers also had no books, except for a few instances.

July 19, 1968—A Guatemalan Co-op Sells Potatoes in San Salvador

I spent the weekend in San Salvador and ran into a Peace Corps volunteer, Jerry, from Guatemala. He had organized a cooperative to help his area's peasants buy fertilizers and other chemicals and to sell their potatoes. He had filled a truck with potatoes and a half dozen of his *campesino* members to go to San Salvador, with the expectation of selling their potatoes at a better price.

He sold potatoes to restaurants for seven dollars a hundred-weight and for six dollars and forty cents per hundred-weight in grocery stores. The co-op had bagged the potatoes according to variety, but they had not separated them by size. The buyers asked them to separate the potatoes by size. Jerry promised that on their next trip to San Salvador, they would do so. Jerry was a lawyer and Yale graduate from New York City, so I thought he did a respectable job for his first attempt.

The co-op members admitted they knew little about potato production. They planted their own seed rather than buying disease-free and treated seed. They applied little fertilizer and used insecticides sparingly. Their soils were sandy and located mostly on steep hillside slopes at eight thousand feet elevation. Jerry told me that he could not find good technical advice in his area of Guatemala. He had the idea that I should visit him to determine if I could give advice.

Jerry said he would wait two weeks before soliciting my services from the Guatemala Peace Corps office. He asked that I visit him as soon as he could make the arrangements. I also put in a request from my Peace Corps office.

July 29, 1968—The Salvadorian Vet Borrows Money from Everyone

Don Napoleón, the teacher shot while walking home, was back at work, and everyone was glad to see him back in command. The students loved him.

My adult class in the Indian community of Pushtan started with thirteen members but dropped to three or four before increasing again to five or six. I had planned to terminate the group at the end of August, but now I thought of pushing it harder and finding ten good farmers with whom to continue working very intensely through the next year.

We were busy catching up on our reports on our thirty corn demonstrations and five projects that we obtained by using bank credit. It took time to stay ahead in our club work, which included planning another group presentation and doing research in the communities we had worked in this year. We also had to investigate potential new communities to fill out our roster for next year.

We also worked on a program to send female 4-H club members to various schools in the area to learn how to sew, make flower arrangements, type, and perform other skills that could help them earn a living and improve their lives.

We wanted to establish places for both boys and girls to work on poultry farms, so they could learn the intricacies of poultry production. They might find employment in these places, but even if they did not, they could apply a small-scale version of what they learned to their own homes. They could produce on any scale and grow their businesses in their communities.

I had thought about attempting to establish a national school of agriculture for *campesino* boys who had finished the sixth grade. The school could have a four- to six-month term of intensive instruction in agriculture. The students could learn about poultry production and fruit and vegetable production. These topics would be most likely to aid the students in having better lives.

I heard a new story concerning the Salvadorian vet: In our office we had a poor old man who worked as janitor and messenger. He had a tough job. The other staff members seldom complimented him on his work, but everyone felt they could criticize him for every little thing they did not like. He was a meek and slight man. He could not have weighed more than eighty-five or ninety pounds. He had thick glasses. I saw a man who always tried hard. He was seventy or seventy-five years old because his body had been used and abused, but still, everyone felt free to criticize him. He earned twenty-four dollars monthly. He paid twelve dollars monthly for his food, four dollars for his room in the office, and four dollars for his boy's school. That left him with four dollars for everything else. He was trying to just stay alive.

Our veterinarian borrowed twenty-eight dollars from this janitor and refused to repay him. He also owed our secretary's mother one hundred and twenty dollars and refused to pay her, and he continued to be behind on his rent with Doña Maria.

My social life was a zero. There was nothing to do but go swimming, which could become boring. Last week I went swimming four times in six days. No matter what I did, you could assume that it was without girls. The girls I wanted to go out with could not go out without a chaperone. Can you imagine! I never saw a girl alone. It was not her fault. The fault lay with the men of this country. They disrespected girls, so girls had to be extra careful. I asked Celia how a boy ever met a girl under these circumstances. She said that the parents usually knew the social position of the boys' parents. Their children could go out, with chaperones, if their children were of similar social standing.

I deduced that this was the reason she could not go to a movie with me or to dinner. I was a stranger of unknown social standing. I was disgusted with the importance of social standing in all aspects of life in El Salvador. Even so, I could sit on the front steps of the house with Celia and be in a room alone with her, if we sat at opposite ends of the long sofa. Celia always was open and friendly with me, and her mother liked me. Her father was a mysterious man who was seldom at home. He lived on their farm that was a couple of hours away by car from the city. I never had a conversation beyond a few words with him. I thought that he left all the social problems of bringing up a daughter to his wife. His responsibility was to care for the farm. His wife's responsibility was to care for the house in the city and Celia.

I no longer tried to impress anyone. The class distinction here was greater than I had imagined, and I hated it. Yesterday, a rich man told me that the problem with El Salvador was that it had too much Indian blood. I immediately disagreed with him, which shocked the hell out of him. I did not stop there. I told him that the only difference between the *campesinos* and us was money and, as a result, education. If you take away those from us, you will have two more unfortunate *campesinos*. He did not like that inference.

I said that in Mexico, everybody had Indian blood, and they were proud of it. I admired them for that, and they were building a strong nation. The Indians had a more advanced culture before the Spanish overwhelmed them than they did today. To this day, the Indians were being held down. He listened and began to half agree, even though it was clear that he did not agree. When I finished, he changed the subject to his forthcoming trip to Sweden and the girls that he hoped to find there.

I realized that was no way to make friends, but I did not need or want that kind of friend. I disliked people with a superiority complex. I liked the lower-class people here because they were honest, hardworking, and sincere. The *campesinos* were not the ones causing the problems with the Salvadorian women; it was the men who considered themselves to be the *campesinos'* betters, the upper-class men.

August 10, 1968—A Message from Jerry in Guatemala

I received a letter from my Peace Corps friend Jerry, in Guatemala. When I left him, he was still selling his potatoes in the San Salvador markets. The potato buyers boycotted him from the market and threatened to run him out of San Salvador. I did not understand exactly, but he had to return to Guatemala City with half a truckload of potatoes.

I offered to move around San Salvador and take orders from restaurants and markets. He could then load their truck with the required potatoes to meet those specific orders, but he had had enough of San Salvador and declined my offer.

Jerry had spoken with the Peace Corps office in Guatemala. They were still open to my visiting Jerry, but they wanted to delay the trip.

In the Peace Corps, we could terminate our service one month early if it were to attend college. If I did this, it would mean that I was halfway through my assignment. I could not believe it. I had felt that the end of my assignment was so far away that I could not even think about it. Now, I could think about it. I was starting to slide down the backside of my assignment.

Last Saturday I went to Izalco to visit the teachers from the school. We visited a farm, where we drank coconut water all morning. It was so delicious and healthy. It was a wonderful day away from home.

The Joneses and I made plans to go to a beach near the Guatemala border. They only have another two weeks before their assignment is complete. I will miss them. They will return to school in San Francisco. It will be good for them to be in such a stimulating environment. It made me homesick, just listening to them make their plans because I wanted to go home too. They already had their airline tickets. I envied them their excitement, but before I could feel that excitement, I needed to complete my assignment.

August 13, 1968—The Joneses and I Go to a Beach Near Guatemala

When the Jones and I went to the beach, it was really an island sandbar, with a swamp between it and land. We arrived midmorning after walking in the hot sun for two miles after we left the bus. We had to hire a dugout canoe, which, with the help of a push-pole, took us to the sandbar. The trip was absent of sound, as the canoe owner pushed off the swamp bottom. We marveled at the silence. The canoe owner agreed to pick us up late in the afternoon. We had to pay forty cents for transport each way.

On Monday, I went to the school and gave my presentation. We also planted a milo demonstration plot, which consisted of a planting of one-tenth an acre. The students were all excited, as I was. We used hybrid seed and fertilizer. This area did not historically produce milo. The government was trying to introduce it because they thought it was better adapted than corn to the uncertain rains. The Indians will not accept milo as a crop because they have been producing corn for hundreds of years. There are two reasons for this: first, tortillas made from milo taste like sandpaper; and second, unlike corn, birds will feast on the milo until the peasants harvest it, reducing yields drastically. I disagreed with the government. I did not think milo had a future in this region.

We were trying to find ten collaborators in each *cantón* to collaborate intensely with us. If we could change the habits of ten producers in five communities, even if it took three years to accomplish, it could bring profound changes to these communities. If these *campesinos* were successful, other, less courageous farmers should mimic their strategies.

The planting of the milo demonstration took from early morning to two o'clock in the afternoon. As we were preparing to leave, a *campesino* approached me to talk. Six months ago, he had been afraid of using fertilizer. Now, he told me that he had just applied for a loan at the bank to buy an eight-acre plot of land and would use it to produce corn and black beans, using hybrid seed and fertilizer. That made my day.

The Agency for International Development (AID) prepared these technological packages for crops. For example, they gave us packages for everything we would need to plant six hundred square yards (about seventy-by-seventy feet). That package contains hybrid seed, starter fertilizer, and a follow-up fertilizer, plus insecticide. The farmer had to agree to use all the ingredients and follow our instructions to the letter. Some farmers agreed to participate for the free planting materials, but most peasants were serious about learning from the experience.

The old way of doing things—using seed only, without any other input—had out-of-pocket expenses of ten cents and could generate three dollars in revenue. This provided a net profit of two dollars and ninety cents. The new way of doing things required a *campesino* to have two dollars and thirty-five cents for every six hundred square yards—a herculean requirement because credit was not available for crop production.

Most *campesinos* could not read or write; therefore, we had to find a separate way to illustrate the difference between the two ways of production for them. We had to boil it down to something physical. Instead of bar charts, we used two piles of ears of corn. They could see the differences in the number of ears, the size of ears, and the number of kernels for each ear. They understood that comparison. We had to simplify, simplify, and then simplify some more.

Today I visited Pushtan, near Nahuizalco, and instead of four adults at our meeting (like our previous meeting), eleven peasants attended my class. Out of the seven new people, one or two would come regularly to meetings. I was happy because the tree grafts that I had done two weeks ago were successful. I was elated. I had never successfully grafted trees before. I often learned to do something one day, and the next day, I would teach peasant farmers to do it in a presentation. It was scary for me, but I had to build my confidence. I could never allow the *campesinos* to know that I had never done it before.

I have taught classes on pineapple, coffee, banana, and of course, corn and black-bean production. I never would have thought that I would give classes in producing these crops. Here, I had to be receptive to learning new things. I gave these classes in Spanish. By now, my Spanish was quite good. I was far from fluent, but I could always make myself understood.

I walked through a couple of coffee plantations to visit the corn-production areas of two members of our adult group. The first one did not have an official technological package. He had bought starter fertilizer and applied it to nonhybrid corn. The results were horrible. The ears were big but had few kernels. I carefully opened the shucks on an ear and counted thirteen kernels. I then carefully straightened the husks and left the ear in place. When we examined an ear in the US, we reached out and ripped it from the stalk and shucked it. The ear would not be among those harvested at the end of the season, since we had picked it and discarded it; it was lost from production. In El Salvador, wasting an ear was unthinkable. The planting areas were so small that each ear was critical. No one randomly picked an ear before it was ready for harvest. These *campesinos* and their families had felt hunger in their lifetimes, and likely they had felt it during most years. It was never okay to discard an ear of corn.

The next site I visited had two technological packages, one worked by the father, and another worked by the son. They were complete packages. Both sites were beautiful, with tall, evenly spaced cornstalks of similar heights and each with a large ear. The plant populations were as recommended. Examination of the ears revealed that all the rows and kernels were filled out. The farmer and his son beamed with pride. I smiled. I liked my job.

After viewing the corn demonstrations, they led me to view their banana plantation. Last week, I had recommended placing fertilizer at the base of each banana plant. Bananas were receiving special attention from *campesinos* now because they had a competitive price—one penny each. This competitive price was because bananas were susceptible to a disease; should a plant be infected; it would lose the entire production. I was pleased to see that he had already placed a small dose of fertilizer at the base of each plant. I smiled again.

We walked onward to view his black-bean demonstration. It was beautiful, tall, deep green, evenly spaced and of even height. Around his demonstration, this peasant had taken the initiative to plant two rows of black beans using common seed, without the benefit of any fertilizer. These beans had yellow and purple leaves and were of uneven height, with an uneven stand, due to poor seed germination. It was a perfect scenario to emphasize the benefits of AID's technological package. In my presentations, I had been preaching the need for the peasants to always have unofficial experiments, or baseline experiments, to determine which of two practices was better. This was an example. Any peasant could notice the two types of black beans and determine which was better. I was thrice proud.

I had left home that morning at a quarter to seven in the morning and returned at four in the afternoon. During that time, I had been on my feet and walking. I was exhausted and hungry. I had walked more than a dozen miles up and down hills.

August 24, 1968—I Get Sick

I started to feel bad after my meeting with Sonsonate's mayor last night. I walked all the way home without buying an ice cream cone from any street vendors. I often bought more than one, but today, I bought none.

When an ice cream street vendor saw me coming, he opened his little top door on his pushcart, and he started pushing cones this way and that way, as he looked for the kind I liked. When he found it, he replaced the door and shifted his feet this way and that as he waited for me to reach him. When I approached him, he opened the cart's top door and pulled out the ice cream cone that I had recently been buying. The ice cream man would be crushed if I did not buy it. I had to buy it. It was my act of kindness for the day.

As I continued to walk home, I felt weaker and weaker. I was so relieved when I turned into Doña Maria's *tienda* and dragged myself through the front room into my room. I removed my shoes and lay down hard on my cot. Doña Maria saw me come in. She recognized that something was wrong and followed me into my room. She felt my forehead. She ordered me to stay put while she brought me pills to take. She returned with a glass of orange juice and mysterious pills. I took them and finished the orange juice. Sleep came quickly.

August 30, 1968—Casa Clark in San Salvador

I was feeling much better, but the last few days had not been easy. The doctor believed my discomfort had been something I had eaten or drunk on Saturday. After I reached my room last Saturday, I lay for a while, resting, and then the diarrhea and vomiting started. A severe headache accompanied these symptoms. I was unable to eat and could not keep liquids down.

By evening, Doña Maria called a local doctor, who made a house call. He brought liquids that I took intravenously.

By Monday morning, I was able to take the bus to San Salvador to see the Peace Corps doctor. I was nervous about the possibility of having to exit the bus in a hurry and scurry into the coffee plants, but I survived.

Monday noon was the first time I had eaten in two and a half days. The doctor sent me to rest and recuperate at Casa Clark. I was not able to weigh myself, but I know I lost weight. My pants fit loosely, but Casa Clark's excellent food would remedy that.

There was another Peace Corps volunteer there for a similar reason. We went to three movies in two days. It was wonderful seeing the big screen and experiencing the wonderful sound system. We saw *The Planet of the Apes*, *The Fox*, and *The Party*.

We will both return to our respective sites tomorrow. I was sad because Bob and Shirley's group was leaving tomorrow for their homes. I will miss them.

At this point, I had been gone from the USA for only fourteen months. It had not been long, but I already felt disconnected from the USA.

This summer had many interruptions, my trip to Guatemala, my illness, the president's visit, and my colleague's suicide. That made it difficult to stay engaged in my work. Now, my friends, the Joneses, had left, and I had no one to talk to. I had the Mormons, but they had no idea about my work or interest in it, just as I had no interest in their work. I needed to dig in and make myself think about El Salvador more than I thought about home.

In November or December, I will travel to Honduras, Nicaragua, Costa Rica, and Panama. The Panama Canal Zone is a tax-free zone. I want to see if I can save enough money to buy a Pentax camera. All the Peace Corps volunteers are doing it. It makes sense to me. I am having the adventure of a lifetime, and I want good photos to remember it; so far, half of my attempts to take photos have failed. I hope to buy a good wide-angle and telephoto lens. I cannot wait. This dream of traveling through these countries with my new camera helps me to stay focused on El Salvador. It is difficult to wait twelve months to go home, but I can wait two or three months to take an exciting trip, and then I will have only nine months before I can go home. That is how I am surviving twenty-seven months away from home. I break it into bits and survive each bit.

September 3, 1968—I Try to Remain Positive

I was still feeling the absence of my friends, the Joneses. To make matters worse, a pair of Mormon missionaries have also moved on to their next assignment. They rotate to new assignments every three months. We had managed to connect, and now they were gone. We watched movies together at the local theater and consumed great quantities of ice cream, milk, and cookies. I felt I should have offered to show them the other side of town, but they never seemed interested.

Today, I went to the Pushtan *cantón*. I often had walked this path with the Joneses, and now I was walking it alone. The distance seemed farther today. I had placed four black-bean demonstrations there, and I needed to view their progress. To my chagrin, each of the four demonstrations appeared worse than the fields planted with common seed. This was suspicious and disheartening. There could be explanations for what I saw, but I could not think of any. I asked the farmers the usual questions, and I still had no explanation.

The farmers wanted permission to tear out all questionable plants and replant using common seed. I could not allow them to do that, per our agreement with the Agency for International Development (AID), but I wanted to give them permission. The farmers, of course, could have ripped out the plants and replanted the area the moment I turned my back, but they did not. They trusted me, but I understood the risk to them. The failure of one small plot the size of our demonstration plot represented a considerable proportion of their total production. The failure of one plot could place the peasants and their families one step closer to hunger before the next harvest.

I was upset that the government-sponsored plots were not working as planned, but I was even more upset that I had no explanation as to why they were not working. I lamented not having a higher technical education yet. I did not like being unable to explain what I saw.

Recently, I had been sad. There had been so many things that had not worked out as I wanted. Some things involved how I viewed myself as part of the team in Agricultural Extension. I had allowed myself to feel sorry for myself, and I had to stop it.

I decided to look for positive things in my life. First, I had all kinds of fruit and other foods available. I drank a glass of freshly squeezed orange juice every morning. I had pitchers of lemon juice during the day. I bought an oxcart-load of coconuts and drank their milk, two or three coconuts a day, and then I ate the soft and savory coconut meat. The coffee that I drank was out of this world, and the food that Doña Maria fixed for me always was fabulous. I loved the soft eggs and rice for breakfast and the rice and beans with soft, fried *platanos* covered in thick cream at night, sometimes with a small piece of meat. I loved the challenge of learning Spanish. Each month I spoke better Spanish. I was quite good now and could understand everything and could make myself understood without even thinking about what I was going to say.

On Sunday, a member from the latest group of Peace Corps volunteers arrived in Sonsonate. I was supposed to care for him like the Joneses did for me. It was strange—I was the veteran volunteer now. Time was passing. His Spanish was horrible, and he always felt uncomfortable and unsure of himself. Watching his behavior, he reminded me how much progress I have made in one year. I was no longer uncomfortable or unsure of myself. I often did not know what to do, but I was not unsure or uncomfortable. I could walk anywhere at any time and feel safe, even though El Salvador had the highest homicide rate in the world.

September 7, 1968—No News from Jerry

I heard no more from Jerry, the Guatemalan Peace Corps volunteer, about my helping him with his producers' potato problem. I did not think I could do anything to help. My knowledge of potatoes was practical, not technical, and the Guatemalan potato producers' problem was technical in nature.

September 12, 1968—The 4-H Members Were Unruly

I arrived at the office at 7:30 a.m., and no one was there. I sat at my desk in the back of the office and read agricultural literature. As people arrived, they gathered and joked or read newspapers. Finally, the agronomist came. He approached me and wanted me to accompany him to Tres Ceibas. This surprised me. He never asked me to accompany him, and I had stopped going to Tres Ceibas months before. The agronomist had worked exclusively with two brothers there. I stopped going because they would never listen to anything I said. We were supposed to collaborate with the community. That was why we called our work "community development," as opposed to two brothers only in a community.

Vicente, the agronomist, gave all eight demonstrations that we had for that community to these two brothers. He had been doing this for years. That was an incorrect use of resources. If the brothers had learned the advantage of using the recommended technological package, then they should have bought the required materials on their own and freed the demonstrations for other farmers who were not yet convinced of the viability of the recommended technological package.

Vicente was insistent that I go with him. Since he was my supervisor, I had to go, but I made him promise to go with me to the school community, Los Almendros, in the afternoon. They had wanted to talk to him for weeks. Finally, he promised, and we left. This was a community to which we had to walk the entire distance. At a fast pace, it was at least an hour. We walked on the railroad tracks for forty- five minutes and then cut across country for fifteen minutes. It was not an easy place to find. It was hidden among small banana plantations, trees, and small fields of corn and beans.

We returned from Tres Ceibas, and each went on to our residences by noon. We agreed to meet at the office when it opened at 2:00. I arrived at 2:00, and no one was there yet. I waited and waited for Vicente to arrive. He did not. Finally, I had the secretary call his home. He said that it looked like rain, and he was not going. It was the rainy season. It always rained. I left immediately. My objective was to leave early, achieve my goals, and return before the rains started. Had I known that he was not going, I could have left almost two hours earlier. I was not pleased.

América and I left without Vicente. We conducted a couple of farm visits on the way to the school. After the school dismissed, we started gathering the 4-H members together for a meeting. The previous week they had asked me about the possibility of having a raffle. We were addressing that problem this week.

We had a tough time getting everyone into the room, sitting down, not yelling, and not doing anything until the meeting started. For each person who entered the room, two left, often to look for someone who had already left. The students were standing, talking, laughing, and yelling across the room and would not listen to América or to me. The female 4-H president refused to enter the room for unknown reasons. Finally, Don Napoleón entered and gave them a lesson in how they should conduct themselves. His presence restored order—until he left the room; then chaos broke out again.

I was disgusted. Eventually, we convinced the 4-H officers to stand in the front of the room. They stood silently, and the students sat silently. The officers had no idea why we were meeting or how to conduct a meeting. We needed to have more official meetings. We had been meeting unofficially for too long. We gave them the assignment of reading the manual to learn how we should conduct a meeting and to create a list of business items that they wanted to resolve, including the raffle.

We just managed to catch a bus from the school when the rain started. It was brutal. I was safe until I had to leave the bus to walk home. I only needed to walk a half mile, but I might as well have walked from the school all the way home. I was soaked and cold when I reached home. I got out of my clothes, dried myself, and took a shower to warm up.

I had received a letter from Jerry from Guatemala. He wanted me to make a short visit as soon as possible. I needed to travel to San Salvador to discuss this with my Peace Corps director.

September 19, 1968—An Attempt to Organize a Cooperative

I asked our agronomist to accompany me to Pushtan because I needed help. He refused because he could not spare forty cents for bus fare. I asked him a total of three times. He refused three times. I was furious. That was his job. I went alone to the *cantón*.

When I returned that night, I prepared a letter to the University of Nebraska. I asked for application forms for both September 1969 and January 1970. I still did not know when I would go home.

On Tuesday morning, I went to the office to prepare for an excursion of my adult agricultural group from Pushtan to Izalco, where the National

Extension Service maintained a small experimental station. This was a group that our agronomist had refused to help many times. I found the agronomist at the office and told him that I was trying to organize a cooperative at Los Almendros, the *cantón* with the school.

The agronomist was receptive to this challenge. The next day he went to San Salvador and contacted a specialist in cooperatives. He set a date for him to visit Los Almendros on Monday and explain the process to form a coop. I was flabbergasted but happy. Finally, our director was providing leadership.

Our office had been disorganized for a while. Instead of working together, we were all working independently. Finally, América called a meeting, and we all voiced our concerns, face-to-face. We agreed to try to work together instead of independently. My experience was that this would last for a few days and then return to the way it was before, but I would try it.

After our discussion, the agronomist went with me and my group of farmers to the experimental station. He was shocked to find ten farmers waiting for us to take them on the tour. He never believed I had such a large group. This motivated him. This was a group that Bob Jones and I had started with two or three farmers one year ago.

On our walk back, the agronomist promised he would accompany me more often because he had just seen more enthusiasm than he had seen in a long time. He announced that he wanted to start a fish project, a cooperative project, and a soil-conservation project. I could not believe my ears. Our agronomist had understood clearly at last.

September 24, 1968—El Salvador Has the Highest Homicide Rate in the World

The Peace Corps had received six new agricultural trainees. They were undergoing further training at the National Agricultural Extension Service's facilities in Santa Tecla. The Peace Corps had chosen me as their guide and translator. We slept on army cots in a dorm room. We had afternoons free.

One afternoon, I received a phone call from our Peace Corps office. The secretary had no idea what it was about, but I was to go immediately to the office. I learned that the Peace Corps Guatemala's official had requested that I spend two weeks with Jerry, the Peace Corps volunteer. I would fly out of San Salvador on Monday, September 30, and spend two weeks on site with Jerry in the Indian village of San Juan Ostuncalco.

Last month, I had been in the American restaurant in San Salvador when the painter I had been trying to meet happened to be talking with the restaurant's owner. The owner saw me and introduced me to Oscar Manuel Garcia, the painter. I arranged to buy one painting a month for ten dollars each. I had the right to reject any painting that I did not like. I paid him in advance for the first painting. He was pleased.

Because of my buying one painting a month, I had little free cash. My upcoming trip to Guatemala would be painful for me because they had the most beautiful clothes, blankets, wood carvings, and other things that I had ever seen. And I had no money.

One Monday morning, I learned that over the weekend, one of our 4-H members had been murdered. An unknown assailant wielding a machete had decapitated him and robbed him of less than one dollar.

One weekend in Sonsonate, there were eight murders. Four of them occurred due to a dishonored husband. The husband thought that his wife had cheated on him, so he killed his wife and the man involved. Unfortunately, the man involved was a bus driver, and two innocent passengers were also killed. The other four were killed at the soccer stadium, where there had been a spirited game between Sonsonate and their number-one rival. These games often became a little testy.

El Salvador had far-right political groups and far-left political groups. They called the far-left group the White Hand. A person considered rich by could wake up and find a white hand painted on his front door. The implied message was that he had seventy- two hours to liquidate his assets and divide them among the poor, or dreadful things would happen to him and his family.

One far-right group simply killed people they did not like. There was a pharmacy located three blocks from where I stayed. The pharmacist received many free samples, which he happily passed on to poor peasant

Indian farmers who could not afford medication. For that, the far-right group entered his pharmacy with machine guns and destroyed everything, including the pharmacists. They claimed that the pharmacists had been Communist because he had been giving away free medicine samples to the Indians.

Chapter 8

I Try to Help Jerry in Guatemala

October 5, 1968—I Will Fly to Guatemala to Help Jerry

I left San Salvador by plane for Guatemala City on Monday at 7:30 a.m. Within the hour, I was in the Peace Corps office in Guatemala City. They gave me thirty-two dollars to cover my living expenses in Guatemala and sent me off for two weeks. Since the first bus for San Juan Ostuncalco was at 2:30 p.m., I went to the central market and bought a leather carrying bag and two beautiful all-wool blankets. I envisioned that my children's beds would use these blankets, if I ever had any. I assumed the nights would be cold where I was going and that the blankets would be useful.

At two thirty, a new Greyhound-like bus pulled out of the station. It had huge windows, giving every passenger a view of the panorama as it slid by. To me, the region seemed like Colorado, but there were differences. There was no snow on the mountain peaks. The needy farmers cleared the mountain forests to their tops to plant more potatoes. There were few rocks in the soil; in fact, the soil was sandy.

The peasants in these areas wore a special kind of shoe, on which the toe and heel were open. At first, I could not figure out why they would open the toe and heel for a shoe. Then I walked in the sand and saw the peasants walk. As they did, sand slid out their toes and heels, keeping their shoes sand-free.

Beautiful, fragrant pine trees covered the mountaintops. El Salvador had no pine trees, with minor exceptions. I arrived in Quetzaltenango at dusk, elevation eight thousand feet. It was too late to go on, so I found a cheap place to stay and eat. I was hungry because I had not eaten much that day. I had weighed myself the day before. I weighed 155 pounds. When I started training, I weighed 177 pounds. When we started our work in El Salvador, I weighed 166 pounds, and I had one year left, during which I would lose more weight.

I began to explore the city. As I walked through the streets, I saw two gringos approaching, and I recognized one of them. He was the Mormon who had left Sonsonate three weeks ago. He was waiting for a bus to his next destination. We had a soda together and caught up on the news.

October 6, 1968, Tuesday—I Arrived in San Juan Ostuncalco

I caught the bus to San Juan Ostuncalco the next morning at six thirty. I found Jerry in an Indian language class. Most Guatemalan Indians spoke only a little Spanish and mostly spoke their Indian languages. In fact, if a Peace Corps volunteer arrived speaking only a little Spanish and even if he committed glaring errors in pronunciation or grammar, the Indians mimicked that manner of speech. The Indians always figured that the white guy knew more Spanish than they did. That made it difficult for new volunteers to improve their Spanish. Plus, new volunteers had to learn the local Indian language.

Indian languages varied. There was another Indian village about every five miles. Each village often had different words in their vocabulary for the same thing. If you traveled three or four villages away, they might speak the same language, but much of the vocabulary was different. This made Peace Corps work challenging in Guatemala.

When Jerry's language class ended, we sat to drink a coffee and plan my two-week visit. Then we walked around his village, and he introduced me to people.

He walked toward a steep mountain slope. I followed him. As we started climbing the steep hill, he told me that this hill belonged to the area's voodoo priests. Soon, we saw a man kneeling and praying. We kept our distance but continued to watch him. He was burning something as he prayed.

He saw us and motioned for us to approach him. We did. He was very pleasant and talkative. He spoke of freedom of religion and mentioned that he was praying for improved health. He said he visited the slope daily and always prayed at that spot—that spot belonged to him; no one else prayed there. All the dozens of other spots that we could see around us belonged to other voodoo priests.

He said that each May they had a convention and met on the slope of a nearby volcano. Last May, he claimed that one thousand priests attended. Suddenly, he told us that our conversation was over, and he returned to his praying.

In the afternoon, we visited a nearby cooperative. There were eighteen members present. We discussed production and marketing problems. After the meeting, we established meeting times on Saturday to visit their individual farms. We returned to Jerry's house, ate, and left for another cooperative meeting at 7:30 p.m. in a town six miles away. This area was mountainous; therefore, these six miles had many ups and downs between the two villages, and we were riding bicycles.

Jerry had his own bicycle. He borrowed one for me. As we started our first descent from a mountain peak, Jerry mentioned that my bicycle did not have any brakes or lights. I quickly overtook him on the descent, but luckily, we had a full moon so I could make out where the road ended, and the steep mountain slope began. At the bottom of the hill, the road turned sharply to the left and then sharply to the right before going up another steep hill. I almost tinkled my pants from trying to keep my bicycle on the road, but after forty minutes, we arrived for the meeting. Sixteen enthusiastic cooperative members were present. Our meeting did not end until nine o'clock.

Jerry wanted to show me more of the beautiful scenery that the full moon offered. I accepted his invitation to deviate from our normal path. He turned and started uphill again. The road was so steep that we had to get off and push our bicycles uphill. Once we crested the mountain, the view of the fields in the moonlight was unequaled. We remained silent for a few minutes and admired the view.

We started down the mountain at nine forty-five and reached home at eleven o'clock. We ate and then slept. We were exhausted. It was very cold inside the house, but my newly purchased blankets saved me.

October 7, 1968, Wednesday—Making Field Visits

We were up early and had a modest breakfast of French bread and coffee. Jerry had his Indian language class at six thirty. After class, two retired married missionaries drove by and offered to take us for a ride. We went to a nearby town, where they produced the most beautiful woolen blankets. They were gorgeous, with flawless workmanship, and so inexpensive, but I had no money. As a Peace Corps volunteer, I had become accustomed to that feeling of having to walk away from something that I wanted. That was an important part of the Peace Corps experience. I did it many times that afternoon.

In the afternoon, we went to our third cooperative meeting. We had to travel several miles to this meeting. The first half of the trip involved climbing a steep slope; mostly, I pushed my bicycle. The last half the trip was downhill. I had to be careful to keep the bicycle under my control, which I did, except for the moment when I almost hit a horse. When we arrived, sixteen members appeared. I was impressed with Jerry's organization. He was flawless—the perfect volunteer.

While the cooperative members were finishing business, Jerry and I climbed a mountain to its summit. From there, we had hoped to see the sun setting over the beach, which often one could see from this point, even though the beach was tens of miles away. Unfortunately, we saw dark clouds roll in one thousand feet below our elevation. It was unsettling to watch them from above.

We returned to the cooperative meeting that finished at 6:30 p.m. It was already dark. We grabbed our bicycles and started pushing them up the mountain to the summit. It took an hour and a quarter to reach the summit. We mounted our vehicles and pushed off into the darkness. There were rocks in the road. This made our lives more exciting. If we hit them, they could bend our tires' rims and throw us from the bicycles. We also had to keep from hitting each other and going off the road. It took fifteen minutes to reach our village at the base of the mountain.

We ate and were almost ready for bed by eight o'clock, but first, I wanted to visit the local agronomist. Jerry took me to his house and introduced me. I wanted him to explain the local agricultural practices.

October 8, 1968, Thursday—We Were Almost Caught in a Rainstorm After Jerry's language class and breakfast, he went to another village to see people about a new classroom addition. I accompanied him just to see.

The students attending this school were mostly poor Indian children. Since this area had Protestant missionaries, children wore clothes that this region normally did not see. The missionaries collected these clothes from the United States. I saw one student dressed in overalls. People in Latin America never wore overalls, but there he was. Patches covered his overalls.

On our return to our village, a rainstorm nearly caught us. Traveling in wet clothes would have been horrible. A wet coat did not offer warmth from the season's coldness. The houses did not have heat. I would have no way to dry clothes other than the natural process, which took a long time at the low temperatures that we were experiencing.

I wore a T-shirt, a long-sleeved shirt, and a coat. I wore these everywhere, even in the house. When I wrote letters, I was fully clothed. Shaving was no fun, although that task was not a difficult one, because my beard was barely visible. We bathed by heating a bucket of water on the stove and using a sponge in a dark corner.

October 9, 1968, Friday—We Feasted with the Missionaries

We traveled to the community called The Hope. We ate lunch in the house of a cooperative member. On the way back, a heavy downpour caught us. We stopped cycling and waited under a tree for a bus to come. We flagged it down, had our vehicles loaded on top of the bus, and climbed in for a safe, dry trip back to our village. We returned to Jerry's house at five in the evening. We had half an hour to change into dry clothes and prepare for dinner with the married missionaries.

The missionaries hosted an excellent dinner party. We drank milk and ate mashed potatoes with two kinds of gravy, peas, creamed corn, carrot sticks, coleslaw, white bread, and whole bread with butter, and all the meat we could eat. They also served two distinct kinds of jellies and ice cream. Wow! To heck with the Peace Corps, I wanted to be a missionary.

Later, because they were going home in two weeks, they gave Jerry and me each a pair of warm socks. I felt like we had been honored. The meal we had just eaten must have taken a couple of people all day to prepare. I was thankful for that meal—and still am.

On our return trip, we took the main highway. As we started, we noticed a car parked on the side of the road. The driver smoked a cigarette. Jerry and I found that to be unusual.

That night, I began to feel pains in my stomach.

October 10, 1968, Saturday—I Get Sick

We noticed the police had stopped a truckload of peasant farmers along the highway. Jerry said they were on their way to the coast to pick coffee. The police stopped them because they wanted a bribe before they would release them. The truckers picked this route because its roads were in the worst condition. They thought it was more likely to be free from police patrols.

That morning, my stomach cramps continued, but we had to leave to visit more peasant farmers.

We met four farmers in the community of The Conception. These farmers were ready for change. One farmer discovered that chemical fertilizer obtained better results if spread on the ground with organic matter. This was a great observation because it was based on scientific fact.

In the afternoon, we went to Quetzaltenango for a piece of pineapple pie. By nightfall, my stomach had neither worsened nor improved.

By three in the morning, I had severe stomach cramps. I had to stand and walk around to gain a small degree of relief from the pain. Then the vomiting started, and I was sick all of Sunday. I was unable to drink or eat anything. There were three things available to drink: soda, coffee, or a local tea. I was unable to keep anything down. Even worse, I could not lie down or sit down. I could walk, but I had to walk bent over. During this time, the house was very cold, and I was uncomfortable. It rained constantly.

I became very depressed, and I wanted to go home. I wanted to leave Guatemala and El Salvador. I wanted to be warm again, and not have any pain, and eat and drink whatever I wanted. Finally, at seven thirty in the evening, I was able to lie down and sleep.

October 12, 1968, Monday—More Farm Visits

We left early to visit eight farms which were located at a high elevation and far from our village. We pushed our bicycles uphill for forty-five minutes. Jerry said we were at 9,500 feet elevation. It was misty and cold. We completed our visits and did what needed to be done. We started our return trip at 12:25 p.m. It started to rain when we reached the summit. By the time we reached home, the rain had soaked us.

Chapter 9

Back in Sonsonate

October 13, 1968—Back in Sonsonate

I was so excited to return to Sonsonate and its warmth, paved streets, and my own little room. This was not the coldest part of the year for Guatemala. January and February were the coldest months. It must have been bone-chillingly unbearable then.

Our agronomist did not cover for me in Pushtan, as he had promised, but he did cover once in Los Almendros. He kept one of four commitments for me. That was better than I had expected.

I felt so incapable compared to Jerry. Jerry had everything organized, but then, he had graduated from Yale with a law degree. That would make him much older, more mature, and better trained than I was. When he organized cooperatives, his skills as a trained lawyer might have been more useful than those of a semi-trained agronomist. I was sure that Jerry could talk to experts and pick up the agronomic details he needed to operate a cooperative. Jerry was an excellent volunteer and worth his weight in gold.

October 18, 1968—I Visit the Painter and His Family

I went to San Salvador and ordered another painting. The painter, Oscar Manuel Garcia, and I were becoming good friends. He promised me that I would love the next painting. I knew he would do his best, so I paid his asking price, but now I wanted his best quality. Usually when he needed money, he made a quick-and-dirty painting in one day and gave it to his wife. She walked about the streets in the market, trying to sell it for the best price she could, allowing them to eat that day.

The painter, his wife, and their two young children lived in a poor community. Their children were malnourished—at least that was my opinion each time I saw them. They were underweight and looked sickly. I felt horrible, but there was nothing more I could do. Buying one painting each month left me without financial reserves. It was the maximum sacrifice I could make.

Each time I visited them, he would invite me into their front room and asked me to sit in a soft chair. He then excused himself and disappeared. Moments later, his wife entered from the backroom and greeted me before she rushed into the street. Minutes later, she returned with a sweet roll from the bakery. She went to the kitchen and prepared coffee. Finally, she reappeared with a silver-like tray that held a small cup of coffee and the sweet roll. They gave me the royal treatment. I had never felt more important.

After the formalities were complete, I looked at his new paintings. Typically, I accepted one of them because it was good. I gave him the money for it and authorized the painting for the following month.

One day when I visited, I learned that one of his children had died. The cause of death was from complications from malnutrition. I wished I could have helped more, but I was now struggling myself. I had allocated ten percent of my living allowance to purchasing his paintings. That was all that I could do.

November 26, 1968—Helping the Coconut Lady on the Railroad

We harvested a peanut crop by hand in Tres Ceibas, a labor-intensive endeavor. Personally, I preferred digging potatoes. It was much quicker to fill a bucket with potatoes than with peanuts.

After the owner of the peanuts and I finished the digging, I started my long walk back to Sonsonate via the railroad tracks. It was early afternoon, the sun was lethal, and I was thirsty. In front of me was a lady who carried a basket on her head that held twenty or more coconuts. I wanted to ask to buy one from her, but I did not want to bother her. Setting the basket down and getting it back on top of her head would have been a major enterprise, so I thought to just pass her.

As I approached her from behind, she stopped and started to set the basket down. I helped her with it and bought two coconuts from her. She happily opened them for me. Coconut milk was always so refreshing. I asked her where she was going to sell the coconuts and what price she could obtain. She was very friendly and kind.

Let me break down the economics of selling coconuts in the market. First, to obtain twenty-five coconuts, the woman would have climbed at least six trees and cut the coconuts to the ground. She then would trim the husk from each coconut with a machete to reduce its size and weight. This allowed her to carry more coconuts per trip to the market.

Once she trimmed them, she put them into a large basket. The basket could weigh fifty pounds or more. She carried this basket across uneven ground to the railroad tracks, and then she followed the track at least three miles into town in one-hundred-degree heat. She might spend all day in the city heat to sell the coconuts. For this, she would receive $1.20. Now she had to walk back to her village in the same heat, but now carrying the empty basket.

Chapter 10

My Trip to Panama

December 19, 1968—San Salvador, El Salvador

I had been planning a trip to Panama for months. Now the time had arrived, and I was off. After spending the night in San Salvador, I took an early direct bus to Managua, Nicaragua. After three hours, we entered Honduras. Honduras was semi-arid, poor, and desolate. Two hours later we entered Nicaragua where the vegetation was greener. We arrived in Managua in early evening. I rented a cheap room and ate a cheap meal. My standby meal was always chicken and rice. It was what the workers ate. There was always a huge volume of rice with peas, corn, and chicken. It was the meal with the most food for the dollar.

December 20, 1968—Managua, Nicaragua

I boarded another direct bus to San Jose, Costa Rica. As soon as we entered Costa Rica, we gained altitude. We were traveling in the clouds. The mist was everywhere, and beautiful flowers were everywhere. Droplets of water accumulated on the plant leaves and dropped onto the mossy rocks, where water again collected before it fell to the roadside and ran downhill. This was where a river was born.

The houses were like the small houses in El Salvador, except they painted these houses in bright colors. They planted flowers in the ground surrounding the houses and hung them on the outside walls by rope and planted in dried coconut husks. They were neat and beautiful. They painted their oxcarts in bright colors and in carefully created geometric designs. As soon as we reached San Jose, I rented a cheap room and ate chicken and rice.

The next morning, I took a direct bus to Panama City, Panama. The road from San Jose into Panama was dirt and full of ruts. Once we entered Panama, the road was paved, and we sailed on into Panama City. Again, I found a cheap room and ate chicken and rice.

I was up early and took a taxi into the Canal Zone to buy my new Pentax camera, tax-free. I already knew the name of the store with the best prices. Peace Corps volunteers who came before me had already done the market research. All I had to do was to go to this store and buy the product, which I quickly did and then headed to see the canal.

I was impressed when I first saw the canal. When I looked across the city, I saw a huge ship that looked like it was sailing down a street. It was in the canal. The lock gates were enormous, but the water pumps still filled them quickly.

I took a slow-moving train to the other side of the Isthmus of Panama, to Colón. The train tracks paralleled the canal. There were many ships crossing the isthmus in the canal. Some were gigantic, and others were tiny. The train crossed swamps that must have required much work before they could support a train. Finally, I reached Colón, at the opposite end of the canal. I looked around, took photographs, and returned to Panama City.

I bought my bus tickets back to San Jose, Costa Rica.

December 30, 1968—Traveling to Costa Rica's East Coast

Once we were in Costa Rica, we started gaining elevation until we reached an altitude over eleven thousand feet. I have no words to express how beautiful it was. Costa Rica was a gorgeous country. At last, we reached San Jose. I rented a cheap room and ate chicken and rice.

The next day I wandered the streets, meeting people. So many people were traveling. All North American land travel to South America goes through Central America. There is only one main highway—the Pan American Highway. If you sit in a bar on that highway, you can see the entire world parade by, eventually.

I met a Canadian with an engineering degree who planned to travel for a couple of years. I ran into an American trying to sell his car so he could keep traveling. A married German couple was headed to South America. I met another Canadian with a master's degree in electrical engineering, and we decided to travel together for a few days.

The next morning, we boarded a slow-moving train to the Caribbean coast of Costa Rica and the village of Limón. The train took seven hours to travel 103 miles. It was a *pinga-pinga* train; it stopped for everyone who came out of the cocoa plantations. It stopped for every woman with a container of milk or a basket of fruit. It never went more than thirty miles per hour. But that was what we were looking for—a way to observe out-of-the-way people fulfilling their normal duties. These people were just that; I could not believe how many people could appear at the tracks through miles and miles of cocoa plantations.

Eventually, we arrived at Limón. There people spoke English because of the former slave trade, but most people were of African heritage. They did not speak English as I knew it; I could not understand them. They spoke what had been English more than 150 years ago, but to me, it was unrecognizable. Unfortunately, not many people spoke Spanish. We spent a couple of hours looking around and took the next train back to San José.

The next day, we went to the Costa Rican bullfights. These were different from Spanish bullfights because they never harmed the bull. He became tired and bored, but they did not harm the bull. It usually was people who were harmed.

To watch the bullfight, we had to pay an entrance fee and sit in the bleachers. If we wanted to be *in* the bullfight, we paid nothing and they allowed us into the bullring, where one hundred or more confederate bullfighters accompanied us.

In the center of the ring was a pole. Around the pole was a small pool of water that was about eighteen inches deep. It had a radius of about ten feet. Its purpose was to offer protection to fleeing bullfighters from an angry bull. The hope was that the bulls would not jump a twenty- four-inch wall and jump into eighteen-inch-deep water. My experience was that the bull was not aware of this arrangement. Fighters who were fearful of being hit by the bull could run into the pool in the center to escape, but the bull sometimes followed the fighter into the pool.

To start the fight, the cowboys coaxed the bull into the arena. When he saw the dozens of annoying humans, he quickly became agitated and charged through the bullfighters. On a good day, the bull wounded about one hundred fighters, they took some to the emergency room. On any given day, the bull could seriously hurt from two to four bullfighters, but the bullfighters kept coming back to annoy the bulls. While this was very entertaining, I did not think the amateur bullfighters were very bright. And then I spotted one of my Peace Corps colleagues in the ring. The Peace Corps had given clear instructions to all volunteers vacationing in Costa Rica that were not to enter the ring. Yet there he was, in the ring.

When the bull showed signs of tiring, two cowboys came out on horseback and approached the bull from each side. They roped the bull and walked it out of the arena to the applause of the spectators. This process of walking the bull out of the stadium did not always go smoothly. Sometimes the bull was not as tired as the cowboys thought he was. In one instance, the cowboys were on each side of the bull and were casting their ropes about the bull's head. One cowboy succeeded at lassoing the bull, but the other failed. The bull took off running. Since the cowboy, who had roped the bull's head, and his horse were anchoring the bull, when the bull bolted, he ran only in an arc, effectively clotheslining dozens of bullfighters who did not see that coming.

My Canadian friend had met a Costa Rican family with four daughters, aged twenty, nineteen, seventeen, and fourteen. The Costa Rican family invited him to their home to celebrate the holidays. They lived in a nice middle-class house that they had built themselves. In addition, the girls knew how to cook, sew, knit, clean, and paint beautifully. The family was ultra-talented.

As guests, all we did was sit and watch. It was interesting. The mother stayed in the kitchen, preparing things, along with the older sisters. The younger sisters brought things from the kitchen to the dining room. Lively Latin music was playing, and the girls moved to the beat of the music. They did not walk; they glided but always to the rhythmic beat of the music. I could have watched them all night. They were art in motion. I loved Latin America.

January 1, 1969—My Canadian Friend Continues His Journey

I awoke midmorning and found my Canadian friend packing. He had decided to continue his journey. He had been in Costa Rica for one month. He felt he needed to continue toward South America, or his money would run out before he had traveled to all the points he wanted to see. I saw him off at the bus depot.

I also packed my things and bought a ticket to Managua, Nicaragua. I would go straight back to Sonsonate without any delays.

Chapter 11

My Work in El Salvador Continues

January 5, 1969—A Peace Corps Volunteer Goes Native

I arrived in San Salvador on Friday evening and went to our apartment to rest. I found a couple of colleagues there. We went to a good movie, *The Graduate.*

The next day, as I approached the *tienda* in Sonsonate, I was surprised when someone asked me, "Did they leave you without clothes also?" I had no idea what the person was talking about. I continued to the *tienda*. When I entered the patio in the back, I saw Doña Maria. She seemed nervous about seeing me. Here is what happened:

The previous night, thieves jumped over the patio wall and gained entrance to Doña Maria's patio. They opened the door on the two vets' room and stole all their clothes, money, jewelry, and everything that was not tied down. The vets were asleep and did not awake. They broke into the second room, but it was not occupied and contained nothing. They tried to break into my room, but my lock was too strong for them, and they chose to run. Maybe one of the vets made a sound, but they spared my room from being invaded. This was good because I had my record player, records, and my clothes. I also had my month's one-hundred-dollar living allowance, my trunk, and its contents. Doña Maria said that when she pulled on my room's lock to determine if it was safe, it popped open. That was how close the thieves had been to gaining access to my room. I felt grateful.

The funny part of the story was that the vets awoke to no clothes. They only had the clothes they had worn to bed. They begged the maid for the loan of a bath towel. I was sorry for the Spanish vet, but the disgusting Salvadorian vet deserved it.

Next week, the painter was to have three or four paintings ready for me to view.

One set of parents who lived on the East Coast were worried about their son. He was stationed in northern El Salvador, near Honduras. He had long ago stopped answering letters from his parents. Finally, his parents contacted Peace Corps Washington, DC. They forwarded the parents' concerns to our director's office. She tried calling the Salvadorian agency director for the office in which he worked, but they had not seen him either. Now, our Peace Corps country director was concerned. She sent our doctor to visit him. He located where the boy had previously been living, but no one had seen him for months. By asking around the village, the doctor heard that people had seen the volunteer in and around another village that was far away. There were no roads that led directly there. The doctor hired one of the men to serve as his guide. They drove as far as they could, and then they walked. As they walked, he asked the peasants if they had seen the volunteer.

When the doctor finally found him, the volunteer was dressed like a peasant farmer, with the hat, the white shirt, pants, and the tire sandals. The doctor learned that he had built a house, married an Indian woman, and received credit on a one-acre plot of land that he had bought. The scene startled the doctor. After talking with the Peace Corps volunteer, the doctor retrieved a syringe from his medical bag and filled it with something. Without the volunteer's knowledge, he poked the volunteer. The volunteer immediately slumped down.

The doctor said that he needed a local ambulance to take him back to his car. A "local ambulance" consisted of a thick tree branch with a hammock tied to each end, carried by two men. When the ambulance arrived, they placed the Peace Corps volunteer inside the hammock, and then they wrapped its sides over him to prevent anyone from knowing who they were transporting. When the volunteer woke up, he was on an airplane on his way back to the States. His parents met the *former* Peace Corps volunteer and the doctor at the Washington, DC, airport. What had happened to the volunteer was that he "went native." This happened occasionally.

February 8, 1969—Homesick Again

Yesterday and last night, I was inexplicably homesick. It was a lighter case of homesickness than I usually had. It came on more slowly and was difficult to identify, but now I know it was homesickness. I was missing the cold and the snow, although I still preferred warm weather. One thing that might have contributed to my homesickness was my approaching departure in nine months. At the beginning of my assignment, I could not even think about my eventual departure because it was so far away. Now, I could think about it because the remaining time would pass quickly.

My thoughts were conflicted about returning home. I did not want to leave here. First, I was making progress with both the 4-H and men's clubs and wanted to continue that progress. Second, I had better friends here than I had at the university. I had grown close to Doña Maria, América, and other people. Third, I could not imagine having a job in the States that would be as meaningful as being a Peace Corps volunteer. Fourth, there was no adventure in the States. Central America was nothing but continual adventure. I thought I would die without the adventure I had here. The US is so developed that there is nothing left to develop. All jobs require that we maintain what already has been developed. The fun for me was in developing something, not maintaining what was already developed.

February 10, 1969—I Become Angry with the Extension Agent

I felt like I was exploding. I had so much locked up inside me that it was impossible to unwind peaceably. Normally, when I was upset, I could speak with my friends here and unwind, but my level of anger far exceeded their ability to absorb my built-up steam. I could talk, write, and work, and still I was exploding.

Last year, I could accept the excuse from my extension agent/ director that I was not present during their planning month in January 1968, but I was present when we made plans for 1969. And we had the great meeting where everyone laid down what we expected from each other. From that, we had a general understanding as to how we would work together, but the extension agent did not follow through.

The agronomist refused to take charge of the office. During the last week, he had an excuse for not accompanying us to the field three times. When he failed to join the team, he severely hindered our ability to achieve our goals. Our work was so important, yet so overlooked and so mismanaged. The people we worked with often had children who were malnourished and sometimes dying from malnourishment. They had no land to farm, bad health, and no money. If there was a disadvantage, they had it. We were the only hope of changing their lives. And our agronomist seldom left the safety and comfort of our office.

As time passed, more babies would be born. Families with new babies would have fewer resources than they had had before the new babies were born. The same plate of frijoles would have to be shared by more mouths. I did not know where to start, how to proceed, or how to finish. I was exploding inside. Nothing was going to change for these wonderful peasant people, not their farm size, not their houses, not their education, not their health—nothing.

On Monday night, I was uncontrollably nervous, so I went to see América, my lightning rod, my friend. After discussing my frustration, we agreed that I should not go to work the next day. I told her that I would go to San Salvador to visit with my Peace Corps director.

On Tuesday, I visited with our subdirector. He listened to me intently and silently. When I finished my sad story, he smiled and said, "Congratulations. I hope you will remain that enthusiastic about your work for the next sixty years. Few volunteers ever arrive at that level of passion. I am proud of you."

February 17, 1969—We Start Working Together

This morning the agronomist handed América and me a paper and asked us for our weekly plans. We filled it out and returned it to him, whereupon we discussed it for an hour. We decided we would work on Saturday to make up for lost time, and on another day, we would visit two *cantones*, rather than the usual one per day. I began to feel a little better, although the agronomist would have to show me that he wanted to work with the rest of us, rather than just telling me. I did not trust him at all anymore.

March 25, 1969—Our Office Finally Received Its Own Vehicle

Our office received its own dedicated vehicle. It is an old Dodge panel wagon. And it runs—they say.

March 31, 1969—Holy Week

Today is the first day of the beautiful street carpets. They do this every Easter. On specific paved streets—and ours is one of them—directly in front of each person's house, each house's occupants build a carpet out of sawdust or salt. They dye it and make beautiful paintings, mostly based off Christmas scenes obtained from Christmas cards. They are gorgeous. Then, on the appointed day, they bring a statue of Christ bearing the cross down the street. This statue is large and heavy. It takes ten men to carry it. They stop on top of each carpet while the priest offers a prayer. They do this for every carpet, and there are hundreds of them. It takes a couple of days to complete.

Anyway, the construction of these rugs had commenced. They closed the roads during this process. It interested that even though it was Easter, people chose to represent Christmas scenes more often than any other scene.

I had a bad cold for several days. Everyone else also had a cold. We contracted it the same night. I tried to sleep as much as I could, but that was not possible because it was too hot. The heat will continue until the rains start, in about one month.

I adjusted nicely to our 1956 Dodge panel truck. I no longer walked much. On the third day, the agronomist asked me to deliver something to a community. While on my way, the police stopped me. They claimed my US license was not valid in El Salvador. In fact, it was not valid. They confiscated my license and asked for my passport, which I did not carry with me. They were going to fine me for not carrying my passport. Eventually, they returned my driver's license and let me continue without any fine. Their goal was to invent a fine and hope I paid it in cash. They would pocket it for themselves.

Chapter 12

My Last Vacation

My Last Vacation in Honduras, Belize, and Guatemala

The first leg of my vacation was to travel to southern El Salvador, near the Nicaraguan border, and then turn northeast to visit a Peace Corps colleague, Tom, with whom I had trained. He would be waiting for me in the central market in San Miguel, the third largest city in El Salvador.

The bus that operated from San Salvador to San Miguel was a newer school bus from the US. When they traded used school buses in the US, they were often taken to countries in Latin America and sold to transportation companies. The bus had to be in decent shape because this was a nonstop route between two major cities. If this bus company wanted to be competitive on this route, it had to have a comfortable bus.

The trip took four hours on a paved highway. Everyone had their windows open because it was hot, and the bus offered no air conditioning. The countryside was beautiful. For me, that was all I needed to pass the time. I never tired of staring out the window at the ever-changing landscapes.

When we arrived at the bus station, I took a taxi to the central market. I was worried that I would not connect with Tom. He had told me that he would be buying potatoes because that was his main food in his village. All I had to do was look for a six-foot white guy in the potato section of the outdoor market.

Tom ate only potatoes. He had no refrigerator; in fact, his village had no electricity, except for a couple of hours during the early evening. A small *tienda* had a generator that operated a half dozen lights and a beer cooler every night between six and eight o'clock. By that time, most people were already in bed.

We greeted each other. He said we should seek a taxi to the bus depot. He had completed his shopping. He had eaten a good hot meal with a steak-like meat and vegetables. He had ordered a big banana split, and now, he had purchased fifty pounds of potatoes. We were ready to head to his village, located in the highlands near the border with Honduras.

After a brief wait, a long bus with high guardrails on its roof parked in front of us in the stall assigned to the bus going to his village. A host of people were already waiting for the bus, and they crowded forward, carrying their purchases from the market. One man climbed onto the roof while the other man passed bags and sacks of merchandise to him. The man on the roof grabbed the merchandise, carried each load to the back of the roof, positioned it, and then returned for more. After Tom gave up his potato sack, he entered the bus and motioned for me to follow. We sat in the front.

When every person had their merchandise situated on the roof and had found a seat in the bus, the driver started the engine and closed the door. We were off. We drove across the city and found a road headed northeast. The road started as a two-lane paved road.

We made suitable time, until we turned onto a dirt road. At this point, the driver stopped, looked at Tom, and opened the door. Tom tapped my leg and waved for me to follow him. We climbed onto the roof of the bus and sat at the front, where we could hang on to the guardrails, should the need arise. When we were seated, Tom banged the bus's ceiling twice, and the driver continued our trip.

It was great having the breeze in my face. There was dust behind us but not in our faces. Soon, the road turned sharply upward. It became rougher, and we made slower progress. The bus rocked from side to side as it maneuvered over bumps and holes in the road. We also had to be careful because there were trees growing on each side of the road, with branches growing over the road. We had to take care so that a branch did not knock us in the face, in extreme cases, dislodge us from the bus's roof. It made the time go by faster.

Finally, we turned a corner, and I saw a bell above the treetops, then the church, and finally the village. It was small, even for a village. The church was small and was a faded white color; it had not seen a paintbrush in decades. At the base of the walls was a brown stain, from rain hitting the brown soil and bouncing back onto the church walls and bringing with it brown soil particles.

The town square was more like an extra-wide street. Opposite the church on the town square was the small *tienda*. Tom led me to his house, which was located near the *tienda*. He had a large old key to open a large, flimsy old lock. When Tom opened his house door, it scraped the entire distance on the floor. Its hinges were loose and barely hanging onto the door. Any drunk falling against the door would have knocked the door down. Safety did not appear to be any concern in this village.

I looked at his house. It had an open and weedy patio surrounded by unused rooms. He had strung two hammocks on posts that were used to hold up the covered part of the patio. He had an old dresser where he stored his few clothes. When I had thought of how a Peace Corps volunteer lived, before I joined the Peace Corps, I was thinking of Tom's house.

It was early afternoon and hot. He proposed we take a nap. We both settled into the hammocks, he in his and me in the guest hammock. A couple of hours later, when the afternoon had become less hot, Tom volunteered to show me the village. He carefully locked his front door, and we headed around the *tienda* and down the street, away from the church. He showed me where the market was once a week. A small area was allocated for it, so it must have been small. He said that he occasionally could buy eggs there. He did not like rice or black beans, so he was destined to eat potatoes—boiled potatoes—every day, without even the benefit of butter.

At the lower edge of the village, we turned and followed a path around the edge of the mountain. After a mile or so, he paused at a spot that overlooked the village and the surrounding area. He sat on a rock and motioned for me to do the same. Then, he pulled out a cigarette and lit it. That was when I noticed it was not a normal cigarette. He inhaled and motioned for me to do the same. I turned him down. I could not even smoke normal cigarettes without getting a horrible migraine headache. No smoking for me. I positioned myself so as not to be downwind from where he was sitting.

The sun was quickly setting. The landscape was green, with layers of blue separating us from the green. The blue became darker and darker until we saw no more. Tom put away his stash, and we retraced our steps to the village. Because Tom had no trouble finding the path in the dark, I assumed this was a path he had taken many times.

When we approached the *tienda*, I heard the motor of the generator running, and then I saw the light emanating from inside and shedding light in a small arc outside the establishment. The *tienda* owner had already placed a small table with a white tablecloth and two chairs just outside the door. I imagine that he had seen Tom and I pass his place earlier in the afternoon. He had a phonograph with an old needle playing Latin music on scratched records. Tom walked in and sat down in one of the chairs and motioned for me to do the same. He held up two fingers, and instantly, two cold bottles of beer appeared. Tom was the only person in the village who could afford to buy a beer.

Tom quickly drained the bottle and ordered more. I was a slow beer drinker, but Tom did not wait for me. He lunged ahead, marching to his own music. The empty bottles accumulated under our table. Tom was now singing to the songs as they played on the record player.

I watched what was occurring around us. The light extended only ten feet beyond our table. A dog appeared from the darkness and approached our table, sniffed our feet, and then continued its path. A peasant silently stepped out of the darkness, carrying his machete and a small net containing his lunch container and the gourd he used to carry water. His lunch often consisted of a stack of corn tortillas; if he were lucky, the tortillas would have cheese or refried black beans in their centers.

Then, I heard a horse's hooves clomping on the cobblestones, slow but steady as he came closer under the cover of darkness. Suddenly, the horse stepped from of the darkness carrying a rider. They crossed our field of vision, continued down the street to the lower village, and quickly were swallowed again by the darkness. The steady clomping slowly faded into silence.

At eight o'clock, the *tienda* owner tried to close, but Tom begged for just one more beer. The owner gave in. Tom drank and sang while the *tienda* owner started to put things back inside. He turned off the record player in mid-song as Tom finished his last beer. Finally, we started across the street to Tom's house. The light disappeared, silencing the generator. There was nothing left to do but sleep. Tom did not even have a candle in his house. He knew where everything was and could easily find his way around his house in the dark. I needed a candle, but I had none. I found my hammock, climbed in, wrapped myself into a ball, and slept.

There was nothing left to do in Tom's village. I took the next bus back to San Miguel and caught the first bus to Tegucigalpa, Honduras. I spent the night in Tegucigalpa and caught a bus the next morning to Puerto Cortes via San Pedro Sula. Puerto Cortes laid on the Caribbean Sea.

I arrived in Puerto Cortes at noon. I found a restaurant frequented by local workers and ate chicken and rice. I enjoyed a small, strong, but sweet coffee after my meal. Drinking this coffee gave the meal more time to settle before I continued the day. After minutes of rest, I got up and walked around the port. I saw large ships at dock; at least, for me they were large.

My next task was to find transportation from Puerto Cortes to Belize. I asked around and found a small boat, forty feet long and about twelve feet wide. It was taking shipments of bottled beer and sacks of concrete to Belize. The boat had two crew members—a captain and a worker/cook. Both crew members were shoeless and shirtless. They only wore dirty and ragged shorts. They agreed to take me for two days and three nights for ten dollars. That included the transportation, food, and a bunk to sleep. I signed up immediately.

We left by late afternoon. The sky was clear, and the ocean was calm. I loved sitting on top, watching the waves and listening to the clunk of the old engine. It seemed old and tired, yet I never doubted that the next clunk was coming. An hour before dark, the crew stopped the boat and turned off the engine. One man jumped into the water and disappeared. Moments later, he reappeared with a fish. He repeated this procedure two more times until he had a fish for each of us; then he joined us onboard, and the engine started its clunking again.

The cook started to make rice and cleaned the fish. As soon as he had one cleaned, he threw it into another skillet. Within minutes, the cook called me to the small table to eat. The table was inside the galleon, but I had to sit on a small stool outside the galleon to eat. The spaces on the boat were small. After I ate, the captain ate, and finally, the cook ate. The cook immediately washed the dishes, dried them, and put them away. It was now dark. I sat on deck, but there was nothing to see. There were no lights anywhere, save a pipe that emitted a glow every time the smoker drew from it. The sounds included the waves hitting the boat's hull and the clunking of the motor.

I went below deck to my bunk and tried to sleep, but I found myself slowly becoming seasick. I had to return on deck to avoid becoming sick. Eventually, I became so tired that I went to sleep as soon as my head hit the pillow.

We arrived in Belize on Sunday morning, but the customs office would not open until Monday morning. We had to dock in the bay and stay on board. That was boring. Spending twenty-four hours on a stopped vessel in sight of land was more than I could tolerate. I wanted to continue my adventure.

When I arrived on shore, I found a nice, cheap hotel, where I took a long shower and ate a breakfast of bacon, eggs, and toast. I noticed that Belize had good-quality food, and I enjoyed it. I slept for the rest of the day, got up, ate chicken and rice, and slept all night. My only problem was getting the bed to stop moving back and forth. I had left the sea, but the sea had not left me.

Early the next morning, I bought a ticket to the border between Belize and Guatemala. Even as we left the capital for the rural area, the road was a well-maintained one-lane road with a layer of crushed rock and the bus had empty seats. We had the windows open, and since it had rained the previous night, it was almost cool. We could hold our hands out and touch the jungle as we sped by.

After two or three hours, the bus stopped, and everyone disembarked. The border guards ordered the people to grab their bags and walk across the border. Another bus was waiting for us there. I had never seen the case where the guards did not allow the buses to cross borders, but because the Belizean and Guatemalan governments were not on good terms, this was not possible.

There was an encampment on the inside of the Guatemala border. I found a cheap place to sleep and stashed my suitcases. I grabbed my camera equipment and started walking about. I met a Frenchman who also had a camera. He was traveling around the world. He paid for his trip by taking photographs, developing them, and selling them. He camped out under an abandoned boat near a small nearby lake. I viewed his photos. They were excellent, much better than anything that I had taken. I found it interesting that I spoke no French, and he spoke no English, but we communicated perfectly in Spanish. I loved being able to speak Spanish. There were so many benefits.

The next day I caught a bus to Las Flores (which translates to "the flowers"), a village located on an island in a lake in the middle of the Petén jungle. I arrived at dusk and took a dugout canoe, powered by a motor, to the island. Once there, I looked for a place to sleep and eat.

I learned that I was not supposed to take any photographs of banks, soldiers, or military installations. The problem was with the Communist guerrillas that were hiding in the jungle. They would take photographs of the banks and military installations and then use them to attack the military installations or rob the banks. They needed to rob banks to pay for their activities. They were active all over Guatemala, but they mostly hid in the Petén jungle area. The government was following their activities and interested in anyone who might support their activities.

The next morning, I walked around the island and took photographs. Two soldiers were patrolling outside a bank. When they saw me, they asked me to take their photographs. Why not? I thought. They posed with their weapons in front of a bank, and I took a couple of photographs. In fact, I used up the last film that I had with me. They wanted me to take more photographs, so I kept taking them, even though I had no film. I guess these soldiers had not received the order about not taking photographs in front of a bank.

Once I had seen everything that Las Flores had to offer, I took a bus to Tikal, the famous site where Mayan Indians had built pyramids hundreds of years ago. It took a couple of hours to arrive. I saw a tiny village and the pyramids. Of the people from the bus, I was the only one who headed toward the pyramid area. The rest disappeared into the houses located around the village. I was the only tourist.

I walked around the area and was surprised there were no restaurants, restrooms, gift shops, or anything. There was nothing except the pyramids. I walked to the tallest of them and started to climb the stairs to the top. I was surprised how steep they were. I felt dizzy and leaned forward until my hands reached the steps. I started to climb with my hands outstretched, like a child. I saw a chain secured to the steps on one side. I grabbed hold of it and slowly climbed to the top.

At the top, the surface area was small. I went to its center and stood up. I felt dizzy and had to widen my foot stance to prevent myself from falling. It was high. I looked out over the jungle. I saw other pyramids that the jungle still claimed. They had reclaimed only a couple, with a couple more partially reclaimed. It was a tourist attraction in development.

After a couple of minutes and a couple of photographs, I started to go back down the steps by holding on to the secured chain. Once on the ground, I walked around a bit and did a quick disappearing act into the jungle for a tinkle break, since that was the only choice I had. My thoughts then turned to my egress from Tikal. Since I was the only tourist, I started to worry about how I might get back to somewhere— anywhere.

I found a man walking on a street and asked him when the next bus left. He thought it would be on Wednesday. Today was Monday. I did not see any hotels, motels, *pensiónes*, or empty houses. I was becoming nervous. I took three deep breaths and asked if there was any other way of leaving.

He pointed at a lone truck in town. "The driver usually leaves the village in the early afternoon."

"Where does he live?"

"He most likely lives in one of those houses behind the truck," he said and then turned and continued his journey.

I went to the truck and noticed that it was loaded with roughly cut mahogany planks. I picked a house and knocked. After a few attempts, I located the driver. He was leaving about two o'clock. I negotiated a price and he agreed to it. I was so happy that I never thought to ask where he was going. I assumed he was going down the same road that had brought me into the village. I was wrong.

I was starving. I had managed to only drink coffee with French bread early that morning. It was noon. All I could do was sit on the shady side of the street in full sight of the truck and wait. I dare not miss my only way out of town, but I could not get my mind off my empty stomach.

At two o'clock, the truck driver approached his truck and motioned for me to climb into the back. We were off. He found what looked to me like the same road on which I had come into the village. It was narrow and covered in crushed rock, and both sides were thick with grassy vegetation.

Every few minutes, a man popped out of the growth along the side of the road and stopped the truck. He and the driver negotiated, and then he climbed on back with me. At first, there were only two of us, then three, and eventually there were six or seven of us. The men seemed to enjoy staring at me.

A boy of ten or eleven came out of the bushes, pulling a heavy sack, and stopped the truck. He negotiated with the driver, but it was not for a ride. His sack was full of pineapples, which he wished to sell. I motioned for him to send one up for me to examine. It was gorgeous, huge, and it seemed perfectly ripe. I asked him how much it was. He gave me a price that was equivalent to a dime each. I bought all ten of his pineapples. He passed them up to me, one at a time. I paid for them, and he disappeared into the jungle.

All the men's eyes were on me and my pineapples. They were curious what I was going to do with them, especially since I had no way to carry them, and I had no machete. I asked if any of them would like to share my pineapples. They all did. I asked if one of them could slice one up— they all had machetes on their belts. One volunteered. Those were the tastiest pineapples I had ever eaten. In no more than twenty minutes, we had finished all the pineapples. I was not as hungry as I had been, but the pineapples were acidic, and that much acid in an empty stomach was not an ideal situation.

After two or three hours, the driver pulled into a village and stopped. I asked when he was leaving again.

"I'm not," he said. "The road ends here, and my trip ends here."

I asked myself, *where is "here"?* My gut feeling was not good. There were fewer houses in this village than in the previous village. They constructed their houses from bamboo sides, dirt floors, and grass roofs. The last village had adobe-brick walls covered by plaster and tile roofs. My gut told me that I was farther inside the jungle than I had been and farther from where I needed to go than I was in the previous village. I needed to take three deep breaths.

I learned that they had loaded a small barge on the river with sacks of corn and was leaving within the hour. Again, I did not ask where it was going, but it was pointed downstream, and that had to lead out of the jungle. I found that reassuring. I negotiated a price and paid my fare, but before I climbed on, I needed to try to secure food to neutralize the acid in my stomach. I asked about places to eat. They told me that the village had restaurants, but they had no food.

The eating establishments in this village had food ready at eleven in the morning, and they served food as long as it lasted. When the food was gone, they closed. It was not possible to special order food. They had no menus. I went to a few places; they were all out of food and closed. I was able to find one place with two pieces of two-day- old bread and a bottle of Guatemalan wine. I bought them and headed toward the barge. I would learn that the bread was too hard to eat, and the wine was too bad to drink.

At least a dozen other people already were sitting on the barge. I made my way to the front of the barge and moved three or four corn sacks here and there to create a soft easy chair. I sat down. I was ready for whatever came.

The boat that was to pull us seemed tiny and underpowered, but as it pulled forward and tightened the tow rope, I felt the barge move—slowly at first, but it gave way and followed the little boat down the river that separated Belize and Guatemala. I estimated the number of fellow passengers at eighteen. Most were small-business people. I met a man who carried soda from civilization into the jungle to sell and then took the empty bottles back to where he bought the soft drinks.

He and I talked for hours. We talked about our families and about the Communist revolutionaries. He said they never came into this part of the jungle; we were safe. He also mentioned that he had heard there were ladies of the night in the boat. They were relocating. The pilot did not think they would be safe on the barge, so he shared his boat with them. He must have been a kind person.

Darkness fell upon us. There was no rural electrification, so there were no lights. As we silently drifted downstream, we occasionally passed a peasant farmer's bamboo hut. On one occasion, the peasant had a fire going. I saw a peasant, who appeared to be squatting over an emery board sharpening his machete. The woman in the hut was preparing either corn tortillas, or *pupusas*. *Pupusas* were tortillas that they split down the middle, like two slices of bread. They had inserted something tasty between the two slices and cooked. I loved the *pupusas* with smashed black beans or cheese. The corn tortillas by themselves were uneatable, but adding smashed beans or cheese made them not only eatable but delicious. They stuck to your ribs. I was hungry and wished I had a couple of them to eat.

The sky revealed all its stars. Every star was visible to the naked eye because on this night, there was no moon. I did not understand how the tow-boat pilot was able to see to guide his boat and our barge down the river, but he did.

At 3:00 a.m., the pilot swung the barge into the river's edge, where crew members secured it. They informed us that this was a barge stop. We would leave at exactly 6:00 a.m. They told us that we could order chicken soup if we liked, and we could rent a hammock, if we wished. I ordered chicken soup, as did other people including the ladies of the night.

The barge stop included a grass hut with an outside fire. They had three crude tables with chairs around them. Nearby there were posts placed in ten-foot squares. Each post had from one to four eyelets used to secure a hammock. People who wanted to sleep had rented a hammock and were fastening them to the posts and climbing in. They wrapped the hammock edges around themselves to protect themselves from the mosquitos and the chill of the night.

Two women had grabbed machetes and headed to a small bamboo building toward the jungle's edge. Seconds later, we heard chickens protesting, and then it was quiet. Minutes later, the ladies reappeared carrying two plucked and dressed chickens. They dropped them into the pot that already had water boiling.

I was sitting at a table watching people when the ladies of the night joined me. They did not see many tourists in this area and were curious who I was. I enjoyed talking with them. We talked of our families and of our travels and our dreams. It was refreshing. Later, I did not remember the details, but I did remember that they all seemed so innocent to me, perhaps because we forgot what they did for a living and only talked as normal people talked.

The soup came and I ate with so much gusto that I was embarrassed. I wanted more, but I dared not ask because they had a limited supply, and everyone wanted more. I laid my head on the table to rest. I did not want to pay to rent a hammock for one or two hours. Then, the sun popped up, and it was six o'clock. The pilot called everyone on board—without any breakfast.

Within an hour, I was surprised to see we were leaving the river and entering the ocean. Now, this concerned me again. I knew I should have asked where we were going. I asked my friend, and he told me that we were going to Puerto Cortes, Guatemala, which was near the Honduran border. He said that we would be traveling three hours on the ocean, which was not as steady as the river. I was not fond of traveling in small vessels in the ocean.

We arrived in port at 11:00 a.m. I was happy to be out of the jungle and out of the ocean, and I could shower, eat, and sleep, which I did in that order. I slept the rest of the day. At night I walked around to see the port town; then I ate again, and I slept some more.

In the morning, I caught a bus to Guatemala City and then to Sonsonate. I was home again. That made me happy. I had had enough adventure.

Chapter 13

Almost Home

The Soccer War between El Salvador and Honduras

Shortly after I returned from my last vacation, El Salvador and Honduras had a soccer game. I no longer remember who won, but the rivalry was great, and a fight in a hotel bar resulted in broken glass in a door. For some reason, the world's correspondents thought that this scuffle resulted in the hot war that followed soon after. They were poorly informed.

The real reason for the war was that Honduras wanted to secure its borders. El Salvador was a densely populated country, with land for farming being impossible to obtain. Honduras, on the other hand, had much land and sparse population. El Salvadorians noticed this, crossed the invisible border into Honduras, and rented land. Being hardworking and good farmers, they prospered and moved from renting land to buying land. These farmers had to be good to survive in the difficult conditions that existed in El Salvador. All the lazy peasants had already perished in the struggle to survive. Eventually, there were so many El Salvadorians inside the Honduran border that the Hondurans started to react and complain. At some point, the Honduran government became aware of the problem.

There was a second condition that created the hot war. It dealt with unfair trade policies. I cannot remember which country was complaining; it does not matter. Those two reasons were what started the war, not the soccer game.

I awoke one morning and walked into the street to head for work, and I saw a huge cloud in the distance. I asked Doña Maria what had happened.

She told me that Honduras had attacked El Salvador by blowing up an oil depot in Acajutla. I wondered if my favorite bar was safe. She also said that they had dropped bombs in other places.

The first bomb dropped by Honduras in El Salvador landed in the patio of a house owned by a Honduran. It failed to explode. Most bombs dropped in this short war failed to explode. They had purchased them from the US after the end of World War II as surplus. The bombs were twenty to twenty-five years old. Storing the bombs so long in a humid environment could easily render them useless. The army constantly sent bomb squads to remove a bomb from a parking lot or a highway. The only bomb that I know exploded was the one that caused the oil storage tank to explode in Acajutla.

Once the war broke out, it made the nightly news in the States. Reporters commented that crazy soccer fans had caused a shooting war. The war they were reporting was so far from what I saw that I thought they were describing another war. I thought they were all holed up in a Miami bar and making up their reports as they drank Cuba Libres from the comfort of their hotel bars.

The El Salvadorian public and I were always looking for more news about the war. All national papers produced extra copies and publishing editions twice a day to keep an interested population informed.

They surrounded the airport terminals with sandbags at least five feet high. They placed sandbags at each corner on the roof, with a fifty-caliber machine gun in place. A crew was always on duty.

I heard a story about a Honduran bomber pilot who executed several bombing runs at the airport each week. The plane's engine was not firing on all pistons. It always sounded like each piston's firing would be the plane's last gasp, but somehow, it kept flying. On each trip, he flew over the airport and dropped a single bomb. Time after time, the bombs hit the tarmac without exploding. After each mission, the bomb squad had to dig it out and try to explode it safely. No one seemed to mind. The El Salvadorian air force was not going to expend the energy to shoot him down because he posed no threat. Each flight made by the Honduran bomber created excitement for an otherwise bored military regiment guarding the airport.

My friend Tom lived in a village near the Honduran border. His village's water supply originated in Honduras. The village elders had a meeting and decided they needed to lead an incursion into Honduras to protect its water supply from the Honduran militia. They formed a group of peasant farmers, armed themselves with machetes, and started their mission at midnight. Tom, bored, accompanied them. They went to the pond and saw no evidence of any military activity, so they returned to their village and slept.

El Salvador's National Guard was moving quickly, even unopposed, toward Tegucigalpa. With less than a week into the shooting war, Honduras proposed peace. Their alternative was to wait and have El Salvadorian troops march into Tegucigalpa. The war was over. Both countries returned to their starting positions.

My Sister Sheri Visits Me in El Salvador

In early spring 1969, the former governor to Sonsonate County contacted me. He had a twenty-three-year-old daughter, Ana, and he wanted her to study English in the US. She had already lived eighteen months in San Francisco, but she had met other Latin girls and spoke Spanish with them. Ana did not learn English. He then sent her to the East Coast with the same result. Now, he wanted Ana to learn to speak and understand English. Someone had informed him that I was from Nebraska. He did not think there were Latin people in Nebraska. I understood clearly what he wanted. He wanted to send his daughter to live in Nebraska to learn English.

He was an important man in the region. I needed to take him seriously. I explained that if Ana were to live with my family, she would not encounter other Latin people, nor would she find anyone who knew how to speak Spanish. My corner of Nebraska was not metropolitan. It was farm country, where people expected everybody to work. I explained that my family would expect her to contribute by washing dishes, setting the table, cooking, cleaning, or whatever help they needed. Ana would have to work to fit in.

My new best friend, Don Chepe, accepted all my conditions. My family agreed to host her. She packed her bags and flew to Nebraska. She adapted to life there. We had hired men who ate their noon meal with the family six days a week. One such hired man was a happy- go-lucky retired man who loved to tease and be teased. He took Ana as a special project. He made her feel at home by teasing her and then forcing her to defend herself verbally. She was happy, and she learned English.

When Ana returned home to Sonsonate, someone had the brilliant idea that my sixteen-year-old sister, Sheri, should accompany her. She could live in Don Chepe's house under his protection to repay my family for helping Ana. For reasons unknown to me, my family accepted. Sheri would accompany Ana to El Salvador. This was just before the Soccer War ended.

On the day of their arrival, I went to the airport to meet Sheri. When I arrived and saw all the sandbags around the outside part of the building and on the roof, with fifty-caliber machine guns and their crews scattered about, I realized that I had forgotten to explain that El Salvador was still in a state of war. I should have mentioned that she might see soldiers, sandbags, and machine guns around the airport and on the roads. I thought that she might become nervous upon exiting the plane on the tarmac and suddenly seeing all the guns and military personnel as she walked toward the airport entrance.

I should not have worried. Since she was walking and talking with Ana, she never noticed anything unusual. We returned to Sonsonate, and she lived the life of luxury with Don Chepe's family.

Chapter 14

My Return Home

Preparing for My Trip Home

During my last week in-country, Peace Corps called me into San Salvador for my exit language test. The possible scores were from zero to five. When I had left training, I had scored a 1+, the minimum allowable to remain in the program. They reserved a score of five for college-educated native speakers. A 4+ was as high a score as a nonnative speaker could achieve. I scored a 4+ on my exit exam. I was fluent. I thought in Spanish. I dreamed in Spanish. I was proud of myself.

The last few weeks had been difficult. My leaving created tension between me and my friends. I knew that when I left, I would never see them again, and they knew it too. They were good friends, and I could not imagine a life without them.

I had daily routines that I enjoyed. These routines would change completely when I left El Salvador, and that would cause me consternation. When Americans leave the US to go to another country, and we suffer an adjustment when we arrive, they call this culture shock. Later, when we return home and suffer an adjustment when we arrive, they call this *reverse culture shock*. I had heard that *reverse culture shock* was worse than culture shock. This worried me because I had been living deep inside the El Salvadorian culture.

América and Doña Maria would feel my absence more than my other friends. They were both like my adopted mothers and I their adopted son, especially Doña Maria, who had no children of her own.

By my last night, I had already given away everything I could not take with me, and I had packed my trunk and suitcase. I was concerned how I was going to carry my trunk and suitcase the half mile to the main highway to wait for the bus on the highway's edge. I had my passport and airline ticket ready on top of my trunk. I had hung the clothes I would wear the next day from the chair.

I visited Celia and said my goodbyes. She cried softly. We hugged. I went next door and spoke with Juana and her mother. They were both sad to see me leave. I had spent so many hours conversing with Juana's mother that I knew she would miss me. I spoke briefly with Juana's father, alone. He asked me directly if I was a CIA spy and wanted to know why I was leaving now. I was speechless. He told me that all the men on the street knew that I was a CIA spy, and there was no need for me to deny it; they knew.

Doña Maria closed her tienda. I had never seen her do that. She had promised me a wonderful meal, and she fulfilled her promise. Just the two of us ate a small steak, rice and black beans, and fried ripe plantain with extra-thick cream on top—all my favorite foods. We had orange juice with the meal and coffee after the meal. Doña Maria had purchased an eight-ounce cylinder of aguardiente, which she mixed with orange juice and gulped a shot. I followed suit, and she finished it off. Doña Maria did not typically drink alcohol.

When we hugged and said our final goodbye, she was tipsy and had tears in her eyes, but she was trying not to cry. As soon as she locked herself into her room, I could hear her crying. In the morning, I would leave early, before the *tienda* opened, via the side door to avoid having to say goodbye to her again. I would see none of my friends again. I went to bed sad.

I could not sleep. I tossed, turned, and thought about how my life was about to change dramatically. I wondered if I could manage it.

Before my alarm sounded, I was up and dressed. I grabbed my trunk and suitcase and carried them outside the house. I carried them a hundred feet before setting them down to rest. It was a good thing I started early. Finally, I reached my spot on the highway from where I knew I could catch the Greyhound bus for my last trip to San Salvador. I never enjoyed the view more than I did that day, knowing it was my last.

In San Salvador, I took a taxi to the Peace Corps office and left my luggage. I had to make one last trip to say goodbye to my painter friend, Oscar Manual Garcia. When I approached his house, he saw me, and his wife immediately appeared from the kitchen, smiled, shook my hand, and ran to buy me my last sweet roll. Oscar asked me to sit down. He said he had a present for me. He gave me a small painting as a gift. In fact, it was still wet. He told me to carry it carefully or the paint would smudge. His wife returned, and I drank my coffee, ate my sweet roll, and treasured every minute with my friends.

I returned to the Peace Corps office, but before I grabbed my things, I said goodbye to the Peace Corps director and subdirector. I appreciated their support and help over the last two years. I grabbed my things, found a taxi, and headed to the airport.

I checked my bags and waited for the airline to call my flight. After they called it, I walked across the tarmac to the stairs leading into the airplane. I remembered what I felt as I descended from the plane two years ago. I was a different person now. I entered the plane and found my seat, and I only wished to be left alone. I was excited yet anxious.

My Return to the US after Twenty-Six Months Away from Home

On the first day, I flew from San Salvador to Mexico City to Houston, where my flight ended, and I had to spend the night. As the plane descended and positioned itself to land in Houston, I saw countless mansions and large patches of green lawns. I thought how nice it would have been if my peasant farmers could have had access to the area dedicated to lawns for them to plant and grow food for their families. I knew already that I had just entered a rich country. Any time people dedicated so much land to growing grass that fed no human or animal, and yet the grass received copious amounts of fertilizer, herbicides, and water, the country had to be wealthy. How wasteful and useless! How unfortunate that there could not be a more equitable way to divide land resources among people.

I was fortunate that my family had a friend who lived in Houston, Christine. She met me at the airport and took me to her and her husband's house. She was very conversant and asked questions. I was slow to answer and then only gave brief answers. I was in shock. I did not want to be a rude guest, but I was. I was not accustomed to any of it. The houses were different; the roads were different; there were no people in the streets; the language was different—and I was different. I wanted to speak Spanish because that was the language I normally spoke. I was not used to speaking English.

I had a tough time sleeping. I was in a nice fluffy bed with a fluffy pillow. In El Salvador, I slept for two years on a canvas stretched tightly across two support beams. I had a pillow, of sorts, but it was not fluffy.

In the morning, Christine fed me a wonderful breakfast and took me to the airport. I was grateful for her help and understanding. She likely knew that it was difficult for me and was not offended by my quiet rudeness.

I caught my plane to Dallas, Lincoln, and then Grand Island. I was not looking forward to what was coming. It would be overwhelming. The plane landed and taxied to its position on the tarmac. People exited the plane and walked across the tarmac to the gate. People waiting at the gate greeted those arriving by given them hugs and kisses, and then, together, they moved on. My family searched for a sign from me, but I was still waiting in my seat. I stood only when everyone else had left the plane, and I inched my way forward. I did not want to leave the plane because that would mean that my Peace Corps experience had ended. I was not ready for that. Once I reached the inside of the airport, I saw my family. There were hugs and kisses all around.

We waited nervously for my baggage and then started home. Everyone was talking, except for me. I was silent. All the English being spoken seemed strange to my ears. On the way home, I looked out the window, and I missed the hues of blue and green from El Salvador. I missed the people walking and waiting by the side of the highway. I missed the old school buses that should have been cruising the highway, dropping off and picking up peasants.

Once home, I moved my baggage into my old room downstairs. Because it was Saturday night, Mom had called for a family dinner in my honor. Grandma, Grandpa, and all my aunts and uncles and cousins came. I did not want to be honored. I wanted everyone to leave me alone, but I had to tolerate this because the family needed the celebration. It was good to see everyone, but the talking was unnecessary. My sensory systems were overloaded. There was too much noise, too much talking, and too much commotion. I yearned for my little quiet room in Sonsonate.

At one point I escaped outside and walked around the farmstead. There was a tall pole located in the middle of the farmstead with a bright light that allowed me to walk around the entire farmstead without a flashlight. I walked into the machine sheds and around the steel bins. I drew a deep breath to smell the smells of the old iron junk pile outside the machine shop, where we always went to scavenge for a piece of metal to weld something. All the buildings were just like I had left them; nothing had changed. It was strange to reach out and touch them.

I returned inside the house, grabbed a plate of food, and sat by Grandpa. He was silent, and I was silent, but we understood each other. When people started leaving, I mentioned that I might go into town for a soda. Mom quickly lectured me that I had to be home early so I could go to church the next morning. I was shocked. I had not had anyone tell me what to do in my personal life in over two years. That alerted me for what was coming. I understood now. No one thought I had changed. Everyone assumed that I would pick up exactly where I had left off two years ago, like going to church on Sunday, working on the farm (when I had no land to farm); free labor for anyone who needed help. I would be donating my labor to other people's land and crops. I would need to win my freedom all over again. I was ready for the fights that were coming.

The next Sunday, I had to move into the dormitory at the University of Nebraska in Lincoln. I had to prepare for that. I had not bought any new clothes since I had left home more than two years ago.

I had stored my 1962 Chevrolet Impala that I dearly loved in the back of the machine shed, with strict instructions for my family that I wanted to find it with the same mileage and in the same condition when I returned. On Monday morning, I went to the machine shed, brushed off the dust, and backed my car out of the shed. It seemed different. I drove it to the farm gas pumps and found that it drove like a lumber wagon. I could not believe it. I abandoned it at the pumps and went inside the house. I learned that a "few times" during irrigation, the farm was short a vehicle, and Dad had to use it for irrigation. It had held shovels, even irrigation tubes and plastic dams. They had used it as if it were an old pickup. It drove like an old pickup. I was furious. It was impossible to have any personal things at the farm. Everyone assumed that what one person owned could be used by anyone for anything.

Dad had always been conservative when it came to spending money on cars. He told me that a car for me was not an investment. It was an expenditure. It was something that, once bought, only decreased in value, even if it were not used and did not generate revenue. That was when I became intrigued when Dad insisted on going with me to buy my next used car for school because I refused to accept the 1962 Chevy anymore. He also insisted that we go to the Pontiac dealership in Central City.

When we arrived at the dealership, I told the salesperson that I wanted a good second-hand car for school. Dad winked and asked the salesperson to first show me what they had in new cars. Dad had obviously been at the dealership before and had everything arranged for them to show me a 1969 red two-door hardtop Pontiac Lemans.

I sat in it and found it comfortable and desirable, and the fact that Dad strongly approved added to its appeal. I had saved the money to buy it, but I was accustomed to used cars; in fact, I was used to walking. I had not driven a vehicle during the last two years, except for a few times after our extension office received the old Dodge panel truck. Looking at a new Pontiac was too much for me. I did not feel comfortable with it, but Dad was so happy. I could not take this moment from him, so I bought it. Dad was ecstatic. I now understand that Dad was proud of what I had done, and he wanted to reward me.

I moved into the university dormitory on Sunday afternoon, eight days after leaving my life in El Salvador. The dormitory had thirteen floors with fifty rooms per floor and two people per room, which amounts to 1,300 immature male students living in one building. Next door was an all-female dormitory, with rooms for 650 females. The two dormitories shared a cafeteria that was located between the two buildings.

The buildings were new and were in excellent condition. The rooms were small but adequate; in fact, I had more space in my dormitory room than I had in my room in El Salvador. They designed the bed, desk, and bookcase to be efficiently adequate. The food was excellent. For breakfast, we had our choice of bacon, sausage, eggs, toast, and a host of other goodies. The cafeteria offered us meat, mashed potatoes with gravy, and our choice of salads, and I could eat cake and ice cream every day. In El Salvador, I had never eaten cake. I was ready to start my junior year.

I soon learned that I had a good roommate, and my courses were challenging. I was happy, although I kept to myself. I found most people uninteresting, even antagonistic. In class, I once overheard a conversation between a couple of guys. The gist of it was that one boy had blown the engine in his car while showing off in the street. He was telling his friend that his father had better replace it with an improved one soon. My only thought was that this was a young person who had not been spanked enough. I overheard other conversations that were in the same vein, spoken by spoiled and entitled children.

I also overheard conversations in the cafeteria line. Guys complained about the horrible food, which they referred to as pure garbage. They said they could not wait to visit home so they could eat a respectable meal again. I boiled inside. I quickly resented these arrogant, entitled children who had something missing in their home education. My reverse culture shock nearly overwhelmed me.

Girls in the cafeteria line had other complaints. They needed a larger allowance so they could buy more dresses, perfume, cosmetics, and other important material items. Inside, I was fuming, but on the outside, no one could detect what I was feeling. One of my female friends in El Salvador had no more than three dresses total in her closet. Both her parents were teachers, a profession that paid little; they had to be very economical. Her parents' top priorities were to keep food on the table and to keep everyone healthy. Their children were all thankful when the parents accomplished this and did not complain about how many clothes they had in their closet.

Little by little, resentment accumulated, and I became hostile to the student population. I did not want to make friends. I did not want to converse with them because they, in general, were immature and spoiled. We had nothing in common. Outside of my dormitory roommate, I lived in isolation.

I had classes and professors that I enjoyed, but a few disappointed me. My adviser was one of them. He taught a class on fertilizers. The exams were fill-in-the-blanks. For example, the question asked might be what percentage of organic matter was in sandy soils; if the answer was 3 percent, and I put 3.1 or 2.9 percent, he counted it wrong because the book had shown 3 percent. He was not practical or flexible. I constantly visited him during his office hours and asked him questions. I am sure he understood that I had become frustrated with his pickiness.

I also shared with him my thoughts from my two years' experience in Central America, including my thoughts on the United Fruit Company. The United Fruit Company was widely known for their people-exploiting practices and their negative impact on the peasants in Central America. I frequently let my adviser know my beliefs on Central American politics and the unfavorable impact that resulted from the United States backing these countries' military and political structures. It always benefited the rich at the expense of the people.

Weeks later, another professor, who was my good friend, warned me to be careful of my adviser. This good friend had been a Peace Corps subdirector in Venezuela. He understood the nature of my reverse culture shock and what I was going through. He said that he had been looking at my folder in Human Resources and saw that my adviser had tagged me as a Communist. I learned that his main investment in his retirement portfolio was the United Fruit Company. I no longer confided in any professors, other than my Peace Corps subdirector friend.

By spring, I was missing all my friends in El Salvador. I missed speaking Spanish. I often found myself thinking in Spanish and still occasionally would start to answer a question in Spanish before catching myself. I was not happy with what I was learning at the university. I was learning facts but not how to solve problems. I did not feel I had acquired any skills that I could take home and use. In El Salvador, I learned to speak a language fluently and how to produce tropical crops. I learned a new culture, a new way of thinking. I felt cheated by the university, and I did not know what to do.

The semester ended, and I returned home to help on the farm. This time, I started out being happy to do the work, since I had not done it for three years. I loved cutting stalks, disking, harrowing, operating a scraper, and all the other tasks. Performing these tasks provided immediate reward. As the machine and I crept across the field, the field became transformed. Every day that I operated the scraper, at the end of the day, I had cut off a high spot and filled in a low spot. I saw the benefits from my work. During the two years I spent in El Salvador, any reward from our work was rarely, if ever, visible.

Eventually, hilling corn—the process of opening little ditches between the rows of corn so that water released at the high end of the field could flow by gravity to the low end of the field—started. One day, I was hilling in a quarter section of corn that was at least four feet high. A quarter section consists of a field that is one-half mile by one- half mile. I had to finish it quickly because, with the elevated temperature and bright sun, the corn was growing rapidly. Under such conditions, corn could grow more than an inch a day. If this corn grew a couple of more inches before I finished hilling, the extra growth could cause stalk breakage by the tractor passing over the stalks, and that would damage the ultimate yield.

The corn had a deep, dark, almost black color. On that afternoon, there was a breeze that blew the corn's leaves in all directions. It made the corn rows disappear, which made it difficult to keep the tractor centered inside the rows. The rows were one-half mile long. All I had to do was point the tractor down the correct rows and then keep one hand on the steering wheel. It was so boring. I dreamed. I thought of El Salvador and how I missed it. I was tired of attending the university and not learning what I thought I should be learning. I was unhappy. I knew that to stop being unhappy, I needed to change something.

At lunchtime, Dad picked me up and took me home. While eating dinner, I was quiet, but no one noticed because there was always so much conversion that it was difficult to get a word in. Suddenly, as everyone was finishing their dessert, I told Dad that I was not returning to the field that afternoon. I startled everyone. All conversation ceased. He did not believe that he had heard me correctly. I repeated my statement. He asked me why. I told him that I was going to hitchhike to El Salvador. The hired men decided they were done eating and asked to be excused from the table. And the conversation between Mom, Dad and me grew serious.

Mom reminded me that other people were depending on me to help them. What would they do now? I replied that a good manager faced problems daily and should be able to overcome them. Dad was concerned with my not working anymore and with my hitchhiking. It was not safe, he argued. I compromised and agreed to take a bus. Mom wanted to know when I would come back. I had no idea. She asked about the university.

Would I return for my last year? I told her that I was not happy with the university and did not know if I would be back by then. Now, my parents were not happy, but I felt better.

In the end, I did not return to work that day. I went to the bank and withdrew a safe amount of money for my living-on-the-cheap trip. I bought a bus ticket that same day, leaving town at 6:00 p.m., that would take me to Laredo, Texas. After the hornet's nest I had just kicked at home, I was not going to stay around and be stung. I packed and had my sister take me to catch my bus. My family may have thought that I was crazy and unreliable, but they could not call me indecisive.

My Trip to Mexico City

It was daytime when I arrived at the Mexican border. Our bus stopped and unloaded all passengers. Passengers went through customs and walked across the border, where I bought a bus ticket to Mexico City.

I enjoyed looking out the window while watching the geography change as we proceeded toward Mexico City. I snoozed a little and watched out the window a little. I was excited. I could not wait to see what would happen when I saw my friends in El Salvador again.

In Mexico City, I had to visit the Guatemalan embassy to obtain an entry visa into Guatemala. As soon as the bus stopped, and I claimed my backpack, I hailed a taxi to take me to the Guatemalan embassy. Once there, I found the waiting room for visas. It was packed. I was disheartened at the thought of how many hours it might take to obtain a little ink stamp.

As I waited, I noticed two tall white guys. I thought they were Americans, but I could not be sure. I tried to listen to their conversation, but there was noise in the room. I approached them and asked where they were headed. The shorter one replied that he was an American soldier, headed to join his unit in the Panama Canal Zone. His friend was accompanying him to keep him company and to help him drive. The soldier was taking his car with him because that was often what soldiers stationed in the Canal Zone did.

I asked if they spoke Spanish. They did not. I volunteered to accompany them and translate for them, even help drive—all the way to the Canal Zone, if they needed. They accepted. We were now the three musketeers.

We received our entry visas for Guatemala and took off for the border. We experienced no problems traveling down to the border. Even so, I felt better once we crossed into Guatemala. I was familiar with Guatemala. I thought of Mexico as mysteriously dangerous. Once we entered Guatemala, it was like we were almost home. It did not take long for us to enter El Salvador and to reach Sonsonate. I needed to contact my sister and ask her to send me money because if I went to Panama, I would be short of funds when I returned to El Salvador.

I introduced my travel mates to América and Doña Maria and Celia and Don Chepe. Somewhere along the way, the soldier contracted a bad case of food poisoning, and we had to extend our time in Sonsonate by a few days.

After the soldier improved, we continued our trip to Panama. We passed through San Salvador and were heading toward Honduras when two men stepped out of a coffee plantation and onto the road. One held up a weapon above his head. I thought it best to stop. It was a National Guardsman and a National Policeman. They had been at a wedding and needed a ride to their next assignment, located about an hour's drive from where we were and where, just one year ago, the war with Honduras had started.

I quickly noticed that these two men were hopelessly drunk. In fact, they kept asking me to stop the car so they could buy firewater. They would even buy us a drink, they said. I translated everything to the soldier and his friend. Finally, the National Guardsman begged for a drink. In desperation, he volunteered to let us shoot his weapon, should we decide to help him. When I translated this, my friends thought that was a reasonable trade. As soon as I saw the next *tienda* on our side of the road, I pulled over. The National Guardsman ran to the *tienda* and disappeared inside. After a moment, he walked out again with his head down; he looked as if the world had just cast him a lethal blow. When he reached us, he explained that they could only sell him firewater if he had his own container.

The American soldier said they had a nearly empty whiskey bottle in the trunk. He offered the bottle to the National Guardsman. In turn, the National Guardsman offered to empty the bottle first. As the American soldier handed the National Guardsman the bottle, the National Guardsman smiled again as if he has just been saved by Jesus. As soon as he finished the bottle, the National Guardsman headed back to the *tienda* in a determined manner. When he came out again, he was smiling, and the again the world was right.

We drove farther down the road and found a quiet spot along the road, and we stopped. We were on a road that was climbing a hill. This spot was forty feet above the coffee plantation that lay below. As we crossed the highway, the National Guardsman carried his weapon loosely with one hand. He gave the weapon to the soldier first. The American soldier examined the weapon and looked down the sights. He loaded a bullet into the chamber and fired three or four rounds. He smiled and handed it to me. The American soldier had to show me how to fire it. I pointed at the sky and pulled the trigger in fully automatic position. The barrel kicked up, and I stopped firing. I then pulled and released the trigger a few times to fire one bullet at a time. When we finished, we returned to the vehicle, and within minutes, we dropped our friends at their destination. The National Policeman had to steady the National Guardsman because he was top heavy but humming happily to himself.

After that, there were no more adventures all the way to Panama. Upon reaching Panama, I said goodbye to my friends because the soldier had to report for duty. They entered the American military compound, and I grabbed a taxi to a cheap hotel. The next morning, I caught a bus to San Jose.

I went to a little restaurant to order my chicken and rice. I picked a long empty table and sat. After ten minutes, I had not even received a menu. The restaurant was not busy; in fact, most of the tables were empty. Finally, I started snapping my fingers to call for a waiter. One looked at me with dagger eyes. He grabbed a menu, walked within about ten feet of the table, and threw the menu at me. I had to catch it to keep it from hitting me.

I tried to get his attention again when I was ready to order, but he seemed determined not to see me. I got up and walked toward him. I asked him for draft beer and chicken and rice. He grabbed the menu that I was handing him, and he walked away without saying anything. He returned with my beer, and he flung it at me from the opposite end of the table. If I had not reached out to stop it, it would have slid off the table. It looked like the service in this restaurant was not going to be great that night. I decided that I would not leave a tip.

I ate my chicken and rice and paid for the food. I would not eat there again. The problem was that Panamanians were going through a political movement. They thought the US should leave Panama and give the Canal Zone back to them. As part of this movement, Panamanians hated Americans. That was all.

When I reached Sonsonate, I had less than one dollar in my pocket. My sister Shelli had wired me money. When I went to the bank and found the money, I was elated; otherwise, my future would have been bleak. I rented a room and ate chicken and rice in a little restaurant, where they appreciated my presence.

During the next week, I visited all the villages in which I had worked and saw my friends. After another week of visiting my friends, I had seen that everyone was fine. I felt reassured and was ready to return to the US. I went to San Salvador and bought my ticket home.

Mom and Dad were happy to see me. I had arrived in time to attend my last year at the University of Nebraska–Lincoln. I worked on the farm doing whatever they asked me to do for the rest of the summer. I was at peace, and my parents were happy.

I attended my classes, passed my exams, and received my diploma—in the mail. I did not go to my graduation. I had gone to my high school graduation for twenty-five students and thought it would never end. I did not care to see how long it would take to walk a few thousand students. No, I went to Colorado and climbed a mountain instead of attending my graduation. On Sunday morning, I hiked down to the nearest village and bought an *Omaha World Herald*. They carried the complete list of students who graduated that May 1971. I also bought a six-pack and hiked back up the mountain. After two beers, I checked the paper. I had graduated. Surprise!

Life was good, except I had a problem. When a person graduates from the university, he should know what he wants to do in life. Not me; I was confused from the two years I had spent in the Peace Corps.

The process of reverse culture shock had not yet run its course. I no longer felt at home in the US. People wasted food and were fussy about what they ate. People were often critical of how food tasted. They had never been hungry for more than a few hours. Food always tasted good to a hungry person.

Most people had closets full of shirts, blouses, shoes, shorts, and coats. In El Salvador, I knew people who had two or three changes of clothes at most. Many had only the clothes on their bodies. That was an unpleasant fact. There was no complaining because complaining did not produce more food or clothes.

In addition, I had no confidence in my technical ability as a college graduate. I had had misgivings about what I was learning before I joined the Peace Corps and how applicable it was. When I returned from the Peace Corps, my hope was that the last two years at the university would pull my learning together and make me feel competent. It did not happen. I always went to class. I studied, and I asked questions, but in the end, I had a feeling of disappointment in myself and in the curriculum that I studied. I had always imagined that a university degree provided one with knowledge that could open the secrets of the universe. I was wrong again. Later, I would learn that the university had provided the foundation that was necessary. What I lacked was experience. No amount of technical knowledge can compensate for a lack of experience.

I did not look for a job in agriculture. Instead, I looked for work at the Lincoln Regional Center because I had a friend who had worked there. They hired me to work with boys with emotional problems, aged twelve to seventeen. The boys had serious emotional problems, although they often seemed normal. There was no chance of advancement in that job, but it would give me time to find myself and choose a direction in life that would be more compatible with my personality. I did not feel competent enough to seek employment in the agricultural sector.

At work, we always had to be on guard. When one child became nervous, for whatever reason, he could cause the others to feed on that nervousness. The result could be a sudden shift in the collective mood from one of peacefulness to one of danger. One evening, there were only two of us on duty. They hired my colleague in the same batch as I was. We both had the same experience, and neither of us had verbal control over the patients. We took our group to recreation in the basement. Some patients played basketball, while others played pool, and still others stood around. It was our job to keep everyone engaged. We encouraged the idle ones to find something to do. Suddenly, they tired of our insistence that they engage, and they became angry. Their mood changed quickly, and they raised their voices and became aggressive. From one minute to the next, we were in a serious bind. We had thirteen angry male teenagers ganging up on two inexperienced employees. One boy picked up a couple of pool balls, one in each hand, and started swinging them around, while another couple of boys picked up pool cues and started to bang one end in their other hand. The boy with the pool balls challenged me to make them do what they did not want to do. The others only stared at me to see how I would react.

My colleague slipped into the office and called the second-floor section that managed another group of male patients. As luck would have it, they also had only two employees. It was against state law for either of us to work with fewer than two employees; therefore, he could not legally leave his post to help us. My colleague gave me the unwelcome news as we tried to figure out how to deal with our problem. Before we knew what was happening, our friend from the second floor burst open the entrance doors, which I knew was for show, stopped, placed his hands on his hips, and looked from one boy to another without saying a word. He was a longtime employee and had instant respect from our patients. They surrendered, and we took them all to quiet rooms on the first and second floors and locked them up for the remainder of the shift. I still give thanks for the second-floor employee's help.

I did not like working at the center, but each morning I had a destination and at the end of every two weeks I had a paycheck. It was one way of treading water while I was in my completely confused stage of life.

After six months, I realized that I needed to look for a better job. I began to summarize the strengths and weaknesses of what I had done in the Peace Corps when I worked as an Agricultural Extension agent. I liked doing that. If I was successful at teaching a peasant farmer a new agricultural technique, he and his family were less hungry the following year. That was positive reinforcement. Any work that I did in the US would be to make money for someone. For me, increasing profits for someone was far less gratifying than decreasing a family's level of hunger. I was not interested in increasing anyone's profits. I wanted to decrease hunger. I wanted to work in Latin America.

I started to prepare a work proposal for an agricultural school for peasants to learn the basics of better agricultural practices. I sent this proposal around to various agencies. One day, I received a phone call, but that will be a story for another day

CPSIA information can be obtained
at www.ICGtesting.com
Printed in the USA
JSHW012248281022
32213JS00001B/18

9 781956 742749